AFRICAN CITIES AND TOWNS BEFORE THE EUROPEAN CONQUEST

AFRICAN CITIES AND TOWNS BEFORE THE EUROPEAN CONQUEST

by Richard W. Hull

W · W · NORTON & COMPANY · INC · *New York*

Copyright © 1976 by W. W. Norton & Company, Inc.

FIRST EDITION

Published simultaneously in Canada
by George J. McLeod Limited, Toronto.
Printed in the United States of America.
Library of Congress Cataloging in Publication Data
Hull, Richard W
  African cities and towns before the European conquest.
  Bibliography: p.
  Includes index.
  1. Cities and towns—Africa, Sub-Saharan—History.
2. Africa, Sub-Saharan—Civilization—History.
I. Title.
HT148.S8H85 1976   301.36′3′096   76–16038
ISBN 0 393 05581 7 cloth edition
ISBN 0 393 09166 X paper edition

1 2 3 4 5 6 7 8 9 0

To my loving wife,
Josephine, and my parents

CONTENTS

PREFACE

THIS book explores urban Africa south of the Sahara during the thousand or so years before the era of European colonialism. Until recently, the subject received scant attention from serious scholars. Only occasional references were made in specialized professional journals on the subject of the origins, architecture, and culture of Africa's towns and cities before the European conquest. Not a single comprehensive work on precolonial urban Africa has been published since Basil Davidson's *The Lost Cities of Africa* appeared in 1959. This pioneering study was the first of its kind. Yet for centuries merchants, missionaries, diplomats, and scientists the world over have been fascinated by the beauty and excitement of Africa's urban scene. Scores of books contain their firsthand observations, though lamentably most of these books have been collecting dust on library shelves. Some required translation from Arabic, others were written in a style that would bring ennui to the casual contemporary reader.

In the sixteen years since Davidson's work, a number of major studies have appeared on specific areas, but they are not easily obtainable for students and interested laymen. Moreover, most of them are highly specialized monographs by architects, archeologists, art historians, sociologists, political scientists, anthropologists, and historians. Sorely lacking, however, is a synthesis of their varied research and the diverse eyewitness reports of visitors to Africa's towns and cities before the onslaught of colonialism and industrialization.

This book attempts, in a concise way, to achieve that essential synthesis. It is comprehensive and multidisciplinary in that it explores, analyzes, and compares major urban centers of the sahel, savannas, forests, and coasts at different points in history and in kaleidoscopic fashion. Urban government, economy, society, architecture, clothing styles, the arts, and education are woven together into a single fabric.

This is not a definitive work on urban African history, even though it is unique in its approach. Nor does it attempt to examine every sub-Saharan town and city. Such a monumental task must be the cooperative and coordinated effort of many minds from a wide variety of scholarly disciplines. Rather, I have attempted only to point the way and to emphasize the crushing necessity for a project of that nature.

The elements of urban Africa which made the precolonial town and city unique, so humane and sensible, are fast disappearing. Few would deny that urban Africa today has begun to display those characteristics of Western urbanism which are so undesirable. Crime, prostitution, poverty, social disorganization and anomie have become part of the modern urban scene. Yet there are still many basic elements of precolonial urban Africa that are worth preserving or at least modifying to meet changing demands. It is the intention here to identify them and to bring them to the attention of the reader, who may some day as a planner, architect, economist, politician, or whatever play a role in shaping a new urbanism for the Africa of tomorrow.

This book would not have been possible without the generous assistance and advice of many scholars, colleagues and students. In particular, I wish to thank Ernest Ako, Jr., University of Science and Technology at Kumasi (Ghana); David Aradeon, Faculty of Environmental Design, University of Lagos (Nigeria); Herbert M. Cole, University of California at Santa Barbara; Douglas Fraser, Columbia University; Aminu Ibrahim, Katsina (Nigeria); Graham Irwin, Columbia University; Thomas Livingston, University of California at Berkeley; Reon Meij, Rands Afrikaans University (South Africa); G. J. Ojo, University of Ife (Nigeria); Friedrich Schwerdtfeger, London University; John Sutton, University of Dar es Salaam (Tanzania); and Robert F. Thompson, Yale University.

I would also like to express my gratitude to the library staffs of the University of Ghana (Legon and Kumasi campuses), the University of Dar es Salaam, Makerere University, The Campbell Collection of the University of Natal, the School of Oriental and African Studies of London University, Columbia University, and New York University.

I am also indebted to His Excellency Mobutu Sese Seko, President of the Republic of Zaire, the New York State Department of Education, and New York University—all of whom over the last five years have provided grants for field and archival work in Africa.

New York City   Richard W. Hull
March, 1976

INTRODUCTION

A popular misconception about Africa is that blacks did not build towns and that they lacked the political sophistication and organization to do so. Most Europeans viewed Africans as living in isolated, unstructured bush communities with little or no understanding of architectural design or appreciation of esthetics in town organization. They assumed that what little town life did exist largely resulted from alien—European or Asian—inspiration. Furthermore, outside observers tended to ignore Africa's rich architectural diversity and to describe its peoples' dwellings as monotonous, look-alike mud and thatch structures.

It cannot be denied that most sub-Saharan Africans lived, and indeed continue to live, in small villages and hamlets. Yet magnificent towns and cities flourished as well. And only a minority of Africans were completely unaffected by them.

As a working definition let us describe a traditional, precolonial African town or city as a collective body of inhabitants under the jurisdiction of an elite with political, economic, or religious authority. I would agree with the eminent urban historian Lewis Mumford that sheer numbers of people do not determine a town, or for that matter a city.[1] Rather, we must see a town or city as a *center*, not only of population but of religion, the arts, governance, the military, industry, or commerce. Even this definition does not suffice. Towns and cities must also act as cultural transmitters, for the mark of a truly great metropolitan center is its ability to radiate its institutions.

Medieval Timbuktu and Djenné were important cities of the western Sudan. Their educational and religious institutions (based on Islam) and their architectural forms (clay box-under-a-dome) became prototypes for a multitude of West African savanna communities.

Although the cosmopolitan Swahili city-states of the East African coast did not become powerful transmitters of culture until the nineteenth century, for centuries they had attracted peoples from Arabia, Persia, northwest India, Indonesia (via Madagascar) and the East African interior.

Still, traditional Africans towns and cities were more than mere transmitters: they received and synthesized. Perhaps the Sudanic and Swahili cities came closest to becoming universal centers, or urban synthesizers of a wide array of diverse cultures.

Unlike western European counterparts, African cities and towns were basically agrarian. At least 70 percent of their male residents commuted regularly to outlying farms. In a sense, some cities, particularly those of the West African forests, could be described as village-cities. Their social and political organization almost mirrored that of the outlying rural communities. But they were more than simply large villages. According to A. L. Mabogunje, all weaving, dyeing and sewing in pre–twentieth-century Yorubaland was carried out in towns, not villages.[2] Indeed, many African towns and cities could boast of well-organized, active industries, ranging from weaving to metallurgy.

Some urbanologists insist that an urban agglomeration is not a "town" unless a significant proportion of its inhabitants devote the greater part of their energies to nonagricultural pursuits: namely, to handicrafts or trade. In other words, to qualify as a town a population center must provide specialized services. Although this qualification is a subject of heated debate, many towns and cities we shall explore are in conformity with it.

In conclusion, towns and cities should be defined not simply by size, though it is an important factor, nor by the proportion of people engaged in industrial pursuits. Many great cities achieved fame not as centers of production but as "middlemen" or focal points of commercial exchange. Thus, it is equally important that we define cities or towns by the functions they perform, their capacity for assimilation, and their ability to transmit a new cultural synthesis.

II.

Towns and cities have existed for centuries throughout sub-Saharan Africa. On the east bank of the Nile lay ancient Meroë, some

120 miles north of Khartoum, capital of the modern Sudan. Meroë, founded more than 560 years before Christ's birth, was capital of the black kingdom of Kush.[3] Southeast of Meroë stood the city of Axum, metropolis of the ancient kingdom of Ethiopia. Axum was situated in the northern reaches of the rugged Abyssinian highlands, approximately 120 miles inland from the Red Sea port of Adulis. Meroë, and its rivals Axum and Adulis, flourished on a lively commerce with Ptolemaic Egypt and the classical Mediterranean world.[4]

Westward across the Sahara lay Kumbi-Saleh, a stone-built capital of the ancient Ghanaian empire. Kumbi-Saleh was located on what is today the fringe of the great Sahara desert, in the southeastern corner of Mauritania. This majestic western Sudanic city achieved wide repute in the medieval world and by the eleventh century A.D. contained a population (estimated by Arab visitors) exceeding fifteen thousand.[5] Three centuries later, the small Niger River trading centers of Timbuktu, Djenné and Gao blossomed into important commercial cities of the empire of Mali and, later, Songhay. Afterwards, a number of small cities would emerge on the upper reaches of the Niger in the high grasslands. Kankan, founded at the beginning of the seventeenth century, became a major Niger River city within a century and a half. In 1795 the nearby city of Segu supported a population of around thirty thousand, according to a distinguished European visitor.[6]

Eastward, though still in the open savanna, lay a series of mud-walled cities belonging to the Hausa peoples. Among them, Katsina had achieved a population approaching one hundred thousand at the twilight of the eighteenth century.[7] More than two hundred years earlier, Mande Dyula traders from Mali had begun to draw their caravan routes southward in search for gold, which they hoped to sell to the newly-arrived Europeans on the West African coast. In the process, these dynamic Muslim traders established commercial and intellectual centers on the forest's edge; towns like Bono-Mansu, Bobo-Dioulasso, Begho, and Kong in an area within modern Upper Volta, Ivory Coast, and northern Ghana.[8] On the southern fringe of the savanna, where it begins to grade into the rain forest, reposed the city of Katunga, or Old Oyo, which was supplying thousands of slaves annually to the Dutch at cosmopolitan Whydah on the Atlantic coast. In contrast, Benin city relied more heavily on a brisk trade in forest products. Though of great antiquity, both cities achieved dramatic growth in the late sixteenth and seventeenth centuries as capitals of territorial empires bearing their names. In the late seventeenth century, two more capitals began to enter the limelight, also in response to the European commercial presence on the coast. They were Kumasi, deep in the Akan forest behind the Gold Coast, and Abomey, high on a dry rolling plateau. Kumasi became capital of the Asante Confederacy and Abomey that of the kingdom of Dahomey. Eyewitnesses in the early nineteenth century estimated that the population of each exceeded fifteen thousand.[9] In the humid palm groves of the Niger Delta flourished a number of compact city-republics, each with its own chief and council, though all linked by a common secret fraternity. These dynamic trading towns—Creek Town, Henshaw Town, Duke Town and Old Town—arose in the eighteenth century. Collectively known as Old Calabar, they served as major distribution centers for the Atlantic slave trade.[10]

In west central Africa the kingdom of Kongo revolved around a densely populated capital called Mbanza Kongo. Its urban residents lived on a high protective cliff overlooking the murky Luanda river. European visitors to the city in the late sixteenth century reckoned that its population hovered at the thirty thousand mark.[11] Nearby, the Congo River and its tributaries were dotted with towns of five to fifteen thousand inhabitants. One of the largest, Kinshasa, was founded some time before 1530. By the mid-nineteenth century there were numerous towns sprinkled throughout the northern savanna/woodlands, some with populations over twenty thousand.[12]

Swinging across the continent to east central Africa, one could find still more population centers. Great Zimbabwe, a capital of the Rozvi Mutapa empire, had become one of the most important urban centers south of the Zambesi river by the fifteenth century. The city had expanded quickly between A.D. 1000 and 1500; and by its peak in the mid-fifteenth century it had become the largest of an estimated one hundred fifty to two hundred towns in the area that forms the watershed between the Zambesi and Limpopo rivers. Though extremely influential, Great Zimbabwe never became a populous urban center and its numbers probably fluctuated between a thousand and twenty-five hundred.[13] Most Mutapans preferred a strictly rural life.

Neighboring Songye peoples, also living deep in the central African savanna, chose to reside exclusively in towns. Some of them in the nineteenth century surpassed a thousand in population.[14] And on a tributary of the Zambesi river lay the Kololo capital of Linyati, which, according to Livingstone, contained more than five thousand inhabitants in 1851.[15] Two decades earlier, Bulawayo arose as the capital of the newly-formed Matabele empire, which was founded by Ndebele invaders from South Africa. By 1888, the city could boast of some ten thousand souls, according to eyewitnesses.[16]

Towns in the interiors of East and southern Africa developed later than elsewhere. In fact, large towns did not appear until after the sixteenth century, when people began to organize themselves on the basis of territorial chieftaincy. Yet even then it would be difficult to describe most of them as towns, for they were almost exclusively agrarian or pastoral in function. And as conglomerations of cattle kraals and farmers' huts their expansion was severely limited. Farmers and cattlemen had to live within walking distance of their gardens or pastures. When the population reached a point beyond which the surrounding lands could not support it, a segment of the community had to move elsewhere. Thus, the nature of land tenure in much of East and southern Africa discouraged town development and forced people to live in small villages or in isolated dwellings on individual farms. Still, for more than nine hundred years both areas have supported clusters of stone kraals and mud-walled dwellings. Indeed, widely scattered ruins from Uganda, Kenya, South Africa's veld, and Rhodesia attest to village life dating from at least the eleventh century.[17] Some settlements were of considerable dimensions. The sixteenth-century kraals at Bigo in western Uganda covered an area exceeding five square miles. Engaruka, a cluster of stone-built terraced communities on the slopes of Mount Ngorongoro in northern Tanzania, may have held four thousand farmers in the twelfth century.[18] Nevertheless, until the completion of further archeological work, it must be assumed that these were atypically large human concentrations.

Exciting urban development occurred along the coast of East Africa from the ninth century A. D. By the close of the fifteenth century more than forty distinct, administratively autonomous market towns thrived along the coral-studded coast and on offshore islands.[19] Their architecture and layout, though distinctly Swahili, received early inspiration from the structures of southern Arabia, Mameluke Egypt, and Seljuk Turkey. Some buildings evoked memories of desert palace fortresses constructed in Syria during the Roman occupation.[20]

III.

It would be an exaggeration to assert that towns and cities shaped the destinies of all African peoples. Some societies, like the nomadic Masai of Kenya, were only remotely affected by life in distant urban centers lying beyond their cultural or occupational frontiers. Yet in some areas towns and cities played a crucial role. And the very survival of states depended upon them. For example, the Ghanaian market-city of Awdaghust was a vital emporium in the trans-Saharan trade. Following its conquest in about 1055 by Muslim Almoravids, the entire Ghanaian economy began to collapse. Many factors contributed to Ghana's demise. But not long after the fall of Awdaghust, Ghana lost its role as the preeminent commercial center of the western Sudan.[21] Likewise, the Songhay empire was fatally weakened when its trading emporiums of Timbuktu, Denné and Gao experienced frequent disruption after the Moroccan invasion of 1591 and subsequent military occupation. For the next two centuries, Islamic learning declined and economic prosperity diminished throughout the Middle Niger region. Merchants and scholars in these great Sudanic cities refused to cooperate with their Moroccan oppressors. Quranic schools were shut down and the volume of trade in international markets tumbled. Many learned men faced exile to Morocco, while the mercantile community gradually migrated to the more secure walled cities of Hausaland or southward toward the forest, source of gold and kola nuts.[22]

In similar fashion, the death knell sounded for the sprawling Oyo empire when Ilorin, the northernmost Yoruba town, capitulated to Fulani cavalrymen in about 1824. Ilorin was the doorway to the Oyo empire; and with its capitulation, Islamic political control began to radiate into the Yoruba heartland. Trade from the north was disrupted and the great metropolis of Katunga (Old Oyo city) strangulated. The economic decline of Old Oyo city after the fall of Ilorin weakened its political influence over the Oyo empire. Rulers of surrounding towns, particularly in the suburbs of Old Oyo, boldly asserted their independence. In 1837 Old Oyo city was abandoned, and within a short time the empire itself ceased to exist.[23]

In neighboring Asante, the confederacy began to fragment after British columns firebombed its capital, Kumasi, in 1874. Weakened and humiliated, Kumasi was no longer able to exert authority over other cities and provinces in the Asante confederacy. Without this urban magnet, the state itself ultimately disintegrated.[24]

City-states on the East African coast played an equally vital role. Indeed, there is no question that interior societies were affected by foreign maritime interference in the affairs of such cities as Kilwa, Sofala, Malindi, Mogadishu, Mombasa, and Zanzibar. After the fifteenth century, Portuguese, Turkish, and ultimately Omani/Arab naval conquests in the western Indian Ocean, combined with raids from interior migrating Bantu, upset the delicate trade patterns and snapped the commercial vitality of these city-states. Interior societies could no longer exchange their gold, copper, and ivory for products of Arabia and India. Decline in the coastal city-states spelled stagnation in the hinterland. And the situation did not change until after the early nineteenth century, when Sayyid Said of Oman in the Middle East transferred his capital to Zanzibar and breathed new commercial life into the atrophied city-states. But now commercial vitality derived primarily from a trade in human cargoes. Indeed, Zanzibar city acquired global notoriety as a center for the purchase of human flesh, for a great many slave caravans seemed to converge on Zanzibar.[25]

For their survival, African cities had to provide security, peace, and stability. Without these requisites, they could not attract or hold people. Clearly, the success of a city can be measured by its magnetism. Conversely, a criterion for the failure of a city is its depopulation.

IV.

Even though urbanites comprised only a minute fraction of black Africa's population, they wielded considerable power and influence and played a disproportionate role in the development of many African civilizations. Scholars in the past have either neglected or grossly underestimated the urban factor in African history. It was fashionable for observers to credit the building of cities and the process of urbanization to colonial regimes. Yet the modern metropolises of Dar es Salaam, Tanzania; Mombasa, Kenya; Kinshasa, Zaire; Bulawayo, Rhodesia; Kumasi, Ghana; Kano, Nigeria and many others are not the products of colonialism. They pre-date the era of European overrule, in some cases by many centuries.

[1] Lewis Mumford, *The City in History* (New York, 1961), p. 93. See also a discussion of towns in David Grove, *The Towns of Ghana* (Accra, 1964).

[2] Akin L. Mabogunje, *Yoruba Towns* (Ibadan, 1962), p. 3.

[3] Margaret Shinnie, *Ancient African Kingdoms* (London, 1965), p. 26.

[4] L. Thompson and J. Ferguson, eds., *Africa in Classical Antiquity* (Ibadan, 1969), pp. 55–56.

[5] *Les capitales de l'quest Africain villes mortes et capitales de jadis*, no. 3 (Paris, 1963), p. 16; also, Raymond Mauny, *Tableau géographique de l'ouest Africain au Moyen Age* (Dakar, 1961), p. 482.

[6] Mungo Park, *Travels in the Interior Districts of Africa* (London, 1799), 1:193–94. Raymond Mauny estimates Gao's population at 75,000 in *ca.* 1591; Timbuktu's at about 25,000 in the 15th–16th century. See Mauny, *Tableau*, pp. 498–99.

[7] See Palmer Collection, File No. 219, Jos. See also Oral testimony, Sarkin Bai, Katsina, 20 July 1966.

[8] Ivor Wilks, "The Northern Factor in Ashanti History: Begho and the Mande," *Journal of African History* 2, no. 1 (1961).

[9] See Richard F. Burton, *Mission to Gelele, King of Dahomey* (London, 1893), 2: 320–26; also Edward T. Bowdich, *Mission from Cape Coast Castle to Ashantee* (London, 1819), pp. 304–14.

[10] A. J. H. Latham, *Old Calabar 1600–1891* (London, 1973), pp. 91–103.

[11] Leo Africanus, *The History and Description of Africa* (London, 1896: 1:73.

[12] Jan Vansina, *The Tio Kingdom of the Middle Congo* (London, 1973), p. 155.

[13] Matabele Thompson, *An Autobiography* (London, n.d.), p. 120.

[14] Jan Vansina, *Kingdoms of the Savanna* (Madison, Wis., 1968), p. 29.

[15] I. Schapera, ed., *Livingstone's Private Journals 1851–1853* (Los Angeles, 1960), p. 137.

[16] Thompson, *Autobiography*, p. 120.

[17] James Walton, *African Village* (Pretoria, 1956), pp. 24–51, 72–126.

[18] P. L. Shinnie "Excavations at Bigo," *Uganda Journal* 24, no. 1 (1960): 49–50. See also Roland Oliver, "Ancient Capital Sites of Ankole" (*Uganda Journal* 23, no. 1 (1959), 51–64.

[19] Merrick Posnansky, ed., *Prelude to East African History* (Nairobi, 1966), pp. 104–15.

[20] Peter S. Garlake, *The Early Islamic Architecture of the East African Coast* (London, 1966), pp. 113–16.

[21] Nehemiah Levtzion, *Ancient Ghana and Mali* (London, 1973), pp. 136–37.

[22] J. Spencer Trimingham, *A History of Islam in West Africa* (Oxford, 1970), pp. 144–47.

[23] Robert S. Smith, *Kingdoms of the Yoruba* (London, 1969), pp. 133–41.

[24] W. Walton Claridge, *A History of the Gold Coast and Ashanti* (New York, 1964), pp. 29–43.

[25] John Gray, "Zanzibar and the Coastal Belt 1840–1884," in Roland Oliver and Gervase Mathew, eds., *History of East Africa* (Oxford, 1963), 1:212–53.

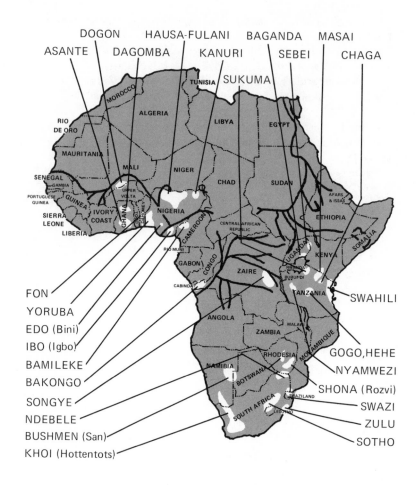

MAJOR CULTURAL GROUPS DISCUSSED IN THE TEXT.

1
ORIGINS OF CITIES
AND TOWNS

I.

IF sizable towns and cities did exist in precolonial Africa, what factors led to their emergence and growth? Most towns grew out of villages; and the process of village-making in sub-Saharan Africa is of great antiquity. Radiocarbon dating has revealed the existence of three-thousand-year-old stone-masonry Neolithic villages in the southwestern Sahara. They surrounded small lakes and were sustained by hunting and fishing and the collection of wild berries and fruits.

Iron technology greatly accelerated the growth of village and town life. Metal tools could be used to fell trees in the humid timberlands. And large human groupings were required for cooperative deforestation. Settlement patterns became more stable with the development of plant domestication and cultivation. The more efficient iron axe, spear, and hoe, together with food plants of higher nutritional value, triggered in certain areas an agricultural revolution which stimulated explosive demographic growth. Surpluses of food and time allowed farmers to devote more attention to governance and the creation of municipal institutions and made it possible to support larger populations.

The Iron Age emerged in sub-Saharan Africa at different periods, in different places, and from a diversity of sources. Certainly, between 300 B.C. and the fifth century A.D. iron-using cultures had begun to replace Stone Age cultures from the Sahara's fringe to South Africa's cool and grassy highveld.

As a prerequisite for town building, societies needed to develop government and leadership well enough to collect, store, and distribute the agricultural surplus created as a result of technological advances in metallurgy and the cultivation of new food plants. It is not surprising that permanent town life developed only after the coming of the Iron Age and the introduction of Asian food crops. Second, leaders had to be powerful enough to demand labor from their subjects for the construction of such public works as royal compounds, markets, roads, religious shrines, and protective walls. Third, a supply of skilled persons was needed to perform these specialized tasks. Fourth, leaders needed to acquire sufficient charisma or power to command rural peoples to support the urban dwellers' dietary requirements. Ideology, expressed in religion and legend, was therefore an essential ingredient. Yet ideology and political centralization did not necessarily lead to the creation of towns. Indeed, some African monarchies deliberately avoided urbanization. For example, although the East African kingdom of Bunyoro had become highly centralized by the late eighteenth century, its chiefs continued to reside in small communities. Bunyoro's leadership remained firmly bound to a rich heritage of seminomadic pastoralism. However, the absence of centralized market activity may also account for the lack of urbanization.

II.

Many towns and cities in Africa originated as spiritual centers. The Hausa city-state of Kano in northern Nigeria sprang from a high rock outcropping, Dalla rock, which had served as the habitation of an important local deity. The priest in charge of the spirit of Dalla rock was basically a religious figure, and his authority radiated more than forty miles in three directions.[1] Between the tenth and eleventh centuries A.D. alien Berbers subverted the local cults and priests in Kano and laid the foundation of a vital center of commercial exchange.[2] Indeed, from that time authority based on kinship relations in settlements throughout Hausaland was replaced by territorial control. Spiritual centers evolved into centralized political units, or city-states, containing inhabitants of diverse origins who lacked kinship ties.

Myths were nevertheless formulated which ascribed the point of origin of Hausa civilization in the city of Daura, which lay just to the north of Kano. According to legend, the Hausa of Nigeria are descendants of a mythical immigrant named Bayajidda, who came from North Africa or the Middle East in about the tenth century. Upon arrival in the village of Daura he slew a snake that had prevented the populace from freely drawing water from the community well. Daura's Queen rewarded Bayajidda with her hand in marriage and ultimately gave birth to a son, named Bawo. After his father's death, Bawo assumed power and produced six sons, who established dynasties in the cities of Kano, Zaria, Gobir, Katsina, Rano, and Biram. The Bayajidda legend, though of doubtful historical accuracy, strengthened Daura's claim as the founding Hausa city-state. Daura never became the political font of the Hausa city-states or an important commercial center. Yet it was recognized by most Hausa people as the cradle of their civilization and the ancestral home of their own ruling lineages.

Great Zimbabwe in central Africa may have evolved in a manner similar to Kano, from the spiritual to the secular. This stone city originated as spiritual center of the Mwari religious cult. Its many monoliths, altars, soapstone birds, and stone tower suggest its role as a vital religious focal point.[3] From the late twelfth or early thirteenth century Great Zimbabwe's leaders gained control of the gold trade and also began to accumulate extensive herds of cattle. Both could be used as a means to amass and measure wealth. And that wealth could command a force of laborers and craftsmen capable of building a city of monumental public structures.

Ife, cradle of Yoruba civilization in western Nigeria, was the spiritual capital of the Oyo empire. According to legend, Ife's founder, Oduduwa, was sent from heaven by God to colonize the earth.[4] Radiocarbon dates indicate that Ife was occupied as early as A.D. 800.[5] From Ife, scions of the royal family fanned out to establish new kingdoms and dynasties. As in Great Zimbabwe, beautiful buildings and works of art were executed to glorify the royal lineage. Today,

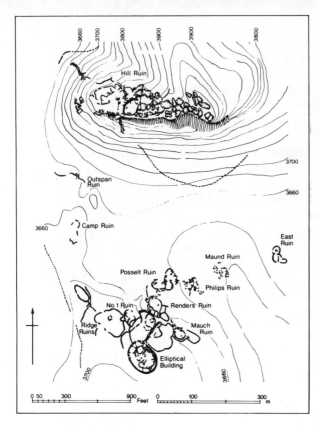

1. Site plan of Great Zimbabwe. The city was composed of three parts: the market which lay within the Great Enclosure in the valley; the surrounding residential area; and the ritual center of the Mwari cult which was situated on the hill. The city, first settled before A.D. 1000, reached its zenith in about 1455 and was abandoned altogether in the early nineteenth century. Courtesy Thames and Hudson, *Great Zimbabwe*, P. S. Garlake, © 1973.

the graceful and naturalistic brass and terracotta sculptures of Ife are world famous. In the past, Ife's art and architecture were emulated throughout Yorubaland. Ife, a spiritual, ceremonial city, was sacred space.

The prevailing urban ethic in spiritual cities like Great Zimbabwe, Daura, and Ife was based not on the expedient mores of the marketplace but on the ritual codes defined by the spiritual leader. Cities of moral order were enduring, though they were often surpassed in size and prosperity by cities governed under a commercial and/or political ethic. Towns serving simultaneously as political, economic, or religious centers were also long lasting. Kumasi, the capital of the Asante confederacy, started out as a marketplace during the time of Obiri Yeboa Manu, about 1633.[6] It was ideally situated between the coast and the great inland trade routes of the Mande Dyula in the northwest and the Hausa in the northeast. These great routes, carrying gold and

2. Scene of the central marketplace at Salaga. By the early nineteenth century Salaga had become the major entrepôt in the West African kola trade. It attracted settlers from the cities of Hausaland and Bornu, who quickly gained commercial supremacy over the Dyula traders who had founded the city centuries earlier. By 1824 Salaga was larger than Kumasi, with a population of about 400,000. The city declined after 1874. L. G. Binger, *Voyage du Niger au Golfe de Guinée*, Paris, 1888.

kola nuts, seemed to converge at Kumasi before flowing to the Atlantic coast. By 1699, Osei Tutu had transformed this commercial crossroads into a politico-religious center as well. It became the repository of the Golden Stool, which symbolized the soul and spirit of the entire nation,[7] and was utilized as a unifying instrument. Spiritual Kumasi was therefore able to cope with threats to its integrity until the British bombardment in 1874.

Katunga, or Old Oyo city, had evolved into a metropolis for much the same reasons as Kumasi. Situated at the southern limits of the savanna, it could regulate movement between the Niger River and the forest. In other words, Old Oyo was in a position to control the flow of trade from the Atlantic coast to Nupe and Hausaland. But Old Oyo was a political city, and it fell with the collapse of the Alafin's (king's)

3. A major wall on the hill at Great Zimbabwe, with pedestals which once supported enormous soapstone birds. Author's photo.

secular authority. By contrast, Ife, its spiritual counterpart, survived the invasions and civil wars of the nineteenth century. And in central Africa, Great Zimbabwe, center of the Mwari cult, flourished as a human settlement from the fourth to the nineteenth century, a period of some fourteen hundred years.

It should be clear that some spiritual centers were transformed into points of secular governance and market activity. Others emerged simultaneously as both governmental and religious capitals. In the early nineteenth century the Hausa city-states were consolidated by the Fulani ethnic group into a theocratic Muslim empire, called the Sokoto Caliphate. Islamic institutions began to dominate the traditional animist cults and an effort was made to create an entirely new spiritual/political capital, called Sokoto city, based on a purely Islamic foundation. Although Sokoto city became the final resting place of Usuman dan Fodio, founder of the Caliphate, and also the capital of the Caliphate until its destruction by the British in 1903, it was never able to enjoy the spiritual stature of Daura, the repository of pre-Islamic Hausa values and ethics.[8]

III.

Towns also emerged where kings and chiefs happened to make their residence. For centuries, successive Kabakas of Buganda staked out their own capital on one of the many flat-topped hills in the vicinity of modern Kampala. The capital, inevitably re-sited by each new ruler, did not contain a central marketplace. People flocked there solely because of its status as the kingdom's administrative and judicial nerve center.[9] Henry Morton Stanley on his approach to the Bugandan capital at Rubaga in 1875 wrote that the capital was situated on the summit of a smooth rounded hill; and at the center of a large cluster of tall conical grass huts lay a spacious, lofty, "barn-like" structure, the palace. Large clean courtyards surrounded the palace, the quarters for the king's harem, and the dwellings of the palace guards. All of these were enclosed by a cane wall, and beyond the wall was a wide avenue parallel to the palace wall.[10] In early Kanem and Mali, capitals were even more mobile and existed wherever the king made his residence at a particular time. These were tent-cities and could be moved quite easily. Many seats of authority in the West African Sudan did not become stabilized until the emergence of permanent market centers.[11]

4. Reconstruction of a kabaka's reed palace in Kampala, Uganda. These structures, once common to Buganda royalty, have disappeared. Author's photo.

But religious or market activity alone was no guarantee of a city's permanence. Numerous short-lived, though important, market-towns of the nineteenth century East African interior grew out of the energies of trader-chiefs like Mirambo, Tippu Tipp, and Kimweri, and through the persistence of Mwinyi Kheri and other Arab caravan operators.[12] These towns developed not as religious or political centers but as provisioning depots and as collection points for caravans of ivory and slaves en route to the coastal Swahili city-states. Ujiji on the eastern shore of Lake Tanganyika emerged after 1830 as perhaps the most important Arab trading town. A European visiting Ujiji in about 1878 observed thirty or more large flat-roofed Arab houses (tembes) with courtyards, broad verandas, and massive walls. These structures were dispersed among a wide variety of traditional African dwellings, including grass beehive huts. Together, they were set within groves of oil palms, banana plants, and fruit trees.[13] Enormous quantities of ivory from eastern Congo passed through its busy markets. Equally important were the neighboring African towns of Urambo and Tabora, which had evolved from clusters of Nyamwezi villages in the

5. Mid–nineteenth-century drawing of Europeans being received by a kabaka in his palace at Mengo, capital of the Kingdom of Buganda. Before 1870, Mengo was a compact and relatively homogeneous ethnic and political unit, situated on four flat-topped hills. John H. Speke, *Journal of the Discovery of the Source of the Nile*, New York, 1864.

1870s. Tabora, in the heart of East Africa and midway between the coast and Lake Tanganyika, became a major point for Arab and Swahili caravans. Towns such as these were places where traders could rest during the rains, replenish supplies, and obtain information on commercial conditions in coastal markets or at the sources of trade further inland.

These communities, as points of converging itinerant traders, were fragile and declined as rapidly as they had arisen. Many were founded by men whose primary concern and preoccupation was trade, not politics. Lacking an institutional base, their fate hinged on the destiny of the individual leadership supporting them. As in the case of Urambo, military force and the sheer personality of their commercial leadership kept the community together.

Commerce and hence town development was further complicated in East Africa by seasonal water shortages and the tsetse fly, which attacked animals and rendered them unreliable as conveyors of goods. Consequently, nearly everything had to be carried atop human heads. Transport was therefore expensive and enormously inefficient. It is not surprising that the high cost per unit of weight carried made it difficult for East Africa's meager resources to compete in world markets. This problem may indeed explain the retardation of East Africa's commercial and urban development, particularly in the Tanganyikan hinterland. Before the nineteenth century town life in that area was virtually nonexistent.

Between A.D. 800 and 1500 a chain of East African maritime city-states evolved as a result of the mingling of diverse ethnic and cultural groups. Some Africanists conjure that Indonesians who had migrated to Madagascar ultimately found their way to the East African mainland from the tenth to thirteenth centuries. If so, they encountered occasional Arab mariners who for centuries had plied the Indian Ocean and traded with still earlier Bantu arrivals from Africa's interior. By the mid-twelfth century larger numbers of Arabs from Oman on the Arabian peninsula and the Shiraz in Persia's gulf had begun to move southward along the African coastline. Unlike earlier Arabs, many of them were political or religious refugees in search of new areas for settlement. Gradually, they infiltrated the small, predominantly Bantu, island and coastal villages. Shirazi immigrants flocked to Mogadishu and Kilwa, which by the thirteenth century had

NEGRO HUTS

6. Panorama of the island town of Zanzibar in about 1873. Zanzibar, one of the oldest Swahili city-states, may have been flourishing as early as the first century A.D. In the fifteenth century it was minting its own coinage and trading actively with cities of the Persian Gulf and beyond. *Graphic*, 1873.

become the two most important mercantile towns on the coast. In each, an Islamic dynasty emerged to regulate the burgeoning trade. Yet Afro-Shirazi success lay chiefly in the capture of Sofala, a busy village along the southern coast. Sofala's markets soon bulged with gold and copper drawn from the interior mines of Mwenemutapa and Katanga. After about 1280, Kilwa's power, culture, and architecture were built upon the profits of the Sofalan trade.[14]

From the fourteenth century a uniquely and highly cosmopolitan Swahili civilization had begun to flower in towns along the coast and on offshore islands from modern Mozambique to Somalia. The urban life was the product of a blending of Omani, Shirazi, and Bantu cultures, cemented together by Islamic religious and political institutions. Each city-state had its own government, ruled through a Sultan, and a council of hereditary elders drawn from leading families. The city-states were autonomous for the most part though they shared a common culture. Ibn Battuta, born in Tangier, visited the East African coastal cities in the early fourteenth century. In 1331 he had this to say about Mombasa and Kilwa:

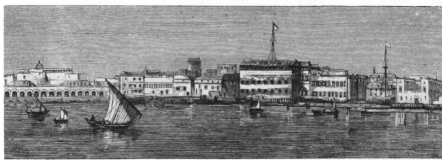

NEW BATTERY   GERMAN CONSULATE   ENGLISH CONSULATE

FRENCH CONSULATE   SULTAN'S PALACE AND ARSENAL

Mombasa . . . grows bananas, lemons, and oranges. The people also gather a fruit which they call jammun which looks like an olive. . . . The people do not engage in agriculture, but import grain from the Swahili. The greater part of their diet is bananas and fish. They follow the Shafi'i rite, [of Islam] and are devout, chaste, and virtuous.

Their mosques are very strongly constructed of wood. Beside the door of each mosque are one or two wells, one or two cubits deep. They draw water from them with a wooden vessel. . . . We then set sail for Kilwa, the principal town on the coast, the greater part of whose inhabitants are Zanj of very black complexion. Their faces are scarred. . . . Kilwa is one of the most beautiful and well-constructed towns in the world. The whole of it is elegantly built. The roofs are built with mangrove poles. There is very much rain. . . . The chief qualities are devotion and piety. . . .[15]

Like the coastal city-states of East Africa, the most enduring cities of the West African Sudan were those whose institutions were firmly rooted in trade. The Niger River market-cities of Timbuktu and Djenné survived the collapse of the Mali empire and continued to flourish as major commercial centers for Mali's successor, Songhay. Along with Gao, these cities had prospered as great middlemen in trade between the forest zone, North Africa, and Egypt. The Niger waterway between Timbuktu and Djenné connected two important

AMERICAN CONSULATE   BISHOP TOZER'S CENTRAL AFRICAN MISSION HOUSE   GAOL

7. Map showing geographical relationship of the medieval Niger River cities of Djenné (Jenné) and Timbuktu. Felix Dubois, *Timbouctou le Mystérieux*, Paris, 1896.

overland routes: the salt route from Taghaza to Timbuktu and the gold route from Djenné (Jenné) to the fringes of the [Akan] forest. Their interdependence is forcefully revealed in an eyewitness African account in 1596. In a description of neighboring Djenné in about 1590 the authority stated

> This city is great, flourishing and prosperous . . . one of the great markets of the Muslim world. Here gather the merchants who bring salt from the mines of Taghaza and who bring gold from the mines of Bitou. . . . It is because of this fortunate city that the caravans flock to Timbuktu from all points of the horizon. . . .[16]

The commercial relationship between the two cities suggests that they grew simultaneously; though Djenné, founded some time between A.D. 822 and 921, is estimated to be two centuries older than Timbuktu.[17] While the prosperity of the two cities was based on long-distance caravan trade, their stability derived from an active local trade in agricultural products. Leo Africanus, an Andalusian Moor born in the North African city of Fez, paid many visits to the cities of the Western Sudan. Of the city of Timbuktu in about 1510, he wrote:

> Here are many shops of artificers and merchants, and especially of such as weave linen and cotton cloth. And hither do the Barbary

8. View of Timbuktu in the mid-nineteenth century. Note the persistence of domical structures among the predominant flat, rectangular buildings. Henry Barth, *Travels and Discoveries in North and Central Africa*, Vol. III, New York, 1859.

merchants bring the cloth of Europe. All the women of this region except maid-servants go with their faces covered, and sell all necessary victuals. The inhabitants, and especially strangers . . . are exceedingly rich. . . . Here are many wells containing most sweet water; and so often as the river Niger overfloweth they convey the water thereof by certain sluices into the town. Corn, cattle, milk, and butter this region yieldeth in great abundance. . . . The inhabitants are people of a gentle and cheerful disposition, and spend a great part of the night in singing and dancing through all the streets of the city. Here [in Timbuktu] are great store of doctors, judges, priests and other learned men, that are bountifully maintained at the king's cost and charges. And hither are brought diverse manuscripts or written books out of Barbary [North Africa], which are sold for more than any other merchandise. [18]

Although the trans-Saharan trade had begun to decline after the Moroccan invasion of 1591, these cities survived. Perhaps they endured, in part, because they continued to serve peasant farmers in the surrounding countryside. Though shadows of their former selves, they have endured to this day.

Thus, the more stable and enduring cities of precolonial Africa developed as a result of intense ritual or market activity. Initially, some cities emerged as collecting points for wandering immigrants who used their favorable locations as spiritual or cultural bases for subsequent territorial expansion. For the Hausa and the Yoruba, Daura and Ife respectively became spiritual springboards for the establishment of expansive civilizations. Other towns and cities, as we have seen, received their initial growth because they lay at the crossroads of commercial exchange.

Many African towns and cities embraced large markets even though they remained agrarian in nature. With the possible exception of the East African coastal city-states, it was common for more than 70 percent of the resident population of any urban center to commute daily to suburban farms. In 1817 an official British visitor to Kumasi, capital of the Asante Confederacy, noted that:

The Ashantees [sic] persisted that the population of Coomassie [sic], when collected, was upwards of 100,000. I say when collected, because the higher class could not support their numerous followers, or the lower their large families, in the city, and therefore

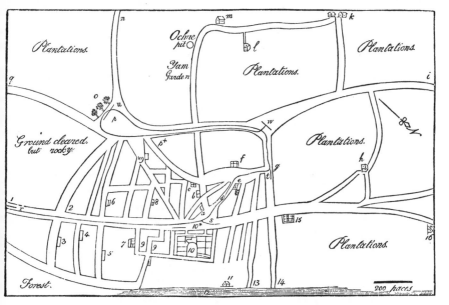

9. Layout of Kumasi, capital of the Asante Union, in the early nineteenth century. Note the straight, broad streets and avenues and the surrounding plantations on the outskirts. Joseph Dupuis, *Journal of a Residence in Ashantee*, London, 1824.

employed them in plantations . . . generally within two or three miles of the capital, where their labourers not only feed themselves, but supply the wants of the chief, his family and more immediate suite. Perhaps the resident population of Coomassie is not more than from 12–15,000.[19]

There is undoubtedly considerable truth to this observation. Moreover, people flowed into the cities during the day to sell their goods in the markets, giving the impression of greater size, and some people lived in the city for long periods following the harvesting of their crops.

Many urban centers were large enough to support well-organized craft guilds. Some towns and cities even gained wide repute for the work of their artisans. The northern Nigerian city of Kano, for example, enjoyed centuries of fame for its leather workers and cloth dyers. A German visitor to Kano in 1851 noted that most of the city's commerce consisted of African products, especially cotton cloth woven and dyed within the city itself. He was later surprised to find Kano cloth selling as far away as Tripoli in the north, Timbuktu in the west, and southward to the Atlantic coast near Arguin. Also found in

Kano's central market were enormous quantities of kola nuts, which when chewed could quench thirst and act as a stimulant, much the same as coffee or tea. Slaves, too, were for sale, along with natron, salt, and other imported items.[20]

In contrast, the cities of Benin and Ife dazzled their guests with naturalistic brass commemorative heads and plaques cast delicately from minerals obtained thousands of miles away in desert mines along the paths to the Nile.[21] Since at least the tenth century several towns in southern Nigeria had enjoyed guilds which cast metal objects through the lost wax process. But few of them were as skilled as the artisans at Benin and Ife.

Trans-Saharan trade, revived by Muslim merchants of North Africa, had sparked urbanization in the West African savanna after the tenth century. Trans-Atlantic commerce after 1500 had a similar effect southward in the forested area and greatly contributed to the growth of the great woodland towns and cities before the European conquest. Likewise, the expansion of Indian Ocean trade after the ninth century stimulated the development of urban life on the East African coast and offshore islands.

10. Entrance to the Sultan's palace at Gedi. Gedi, a medieval East African coastal city-state, was mysteriously abandoned in the fourteenth century. Author's photo.

11. A Gedi doorway leading out of an impluvial courtyard in the inner palace. Walls were made of coral rag and doorway was formed by carefully chiseled blocks of coral. Author's photo.

12. A phallic-shaped minaret, typical of the mosques which were so common in the medieval Swahili city-states. Author's photo.

13. Former Arab mansion in Zanzibar City, probably constructed in the early nineteenth century, when Sayyid Said, Zanzibar's sultan, attracted Arabs from Oman to establish plantations and operate slave caravans into the mainland's interior. Author's photo.

14a and b. Former residences of Indian Banyans. Sultan Said invited wealthy Indian money-lenders to Zanzibar. They provided capital for the Arab and Swahili slave trading operations. Author's photos.

Ironically, war and slave raiding also accelerated the tendency toward urbanization in some societies. By the eighteenth century a series of defensive settlements had appeared from the Gambia to Liberia. Mende new-towns in central Sierra Leone were laid out defensively, surrounded by wooden stockades and stake-filled ditches. By the mid-eighteenth century, some of these war-towns held populations approaching a thousand. Satellite villages, usually lying within a five mile range, supported the townsfolk with food. Another chain of war-towns appeared between 1825 and 1830 in defense against Fulbe and Mane raids. In Sierra Leone and the Gambia, defensive communities were situated on valley slopes or on low-lying hills.[22]

As the Asante nation, in the Gold Coast hinterland, grew territorially from the mid-eighteenth century, it created new towns by transferring war captives to prisoner concentration centers on the confederacy's periphery.[23] These centers, like those that sprang forth in the same period in Dahomey, served as mechanisms for cultural assimilation. The vanquished learned the values, languages, and life styles of their captors. It was an ingenious and surprisingly successful attempt to forge disparate peoples, anomized and traumatized by war, into a homogeneous culture. Once assimilated, they were considered members of the state.

The Yoruba in western Nigeria acquired a propensity for living in large permanent settlements long before the European conquest.[24] This tendency may have been a reflection of the centralized patterns of political authority that had existed since at least the late fifteenth century, before the heyday of the Oyo empire.[25] Yet the Fulani invasions of the early nineteenth century, leading to the collapse of Old Oyo city and civil war, profoundly affected Yoruba urban development. By 1830 Old Oyo's suburbs had become depopulated for some sixty miles as people fled southward.

This demographic dislocation ironically accelerated the process of urbanization. Warrior camps mushroomed everywhere, many of them evolving into large, though amorphous and poorly planned, cities of refuge. New cities emerged, like Ibadan, because of their ability to protect refugees from devastating civil wars and to provide for food and security. Ibadan began in 1829 as an insignificant Egba

15. View of Sikasso, a large city of the Western Sudan which was thrown into the vortex of Muslim military upheavals and empire-building in the eighteenth and nineteenth centuries. Its protective walls were among the most impressive and unusual in West Africa. Sikasso lay along the vital caravan route between Segu, Bondoukou, and the Gold Coast, and was besieged for fifteen months in 1887–88. L. G. Binger, *Voyage du Niger au Golfe de Guinée*, Paris, 1888.

farming village on the edge of the grassland. Its name derived from the word *Idi-Ibon*, meaning "the butt end of a gun."[26] Indeed, its commanding situation on a large laterite outcropping made it an ideal defense against Fulani cavalrymen. Within three decades the quiet village had grown into the most powerful city in Yorubaland, with a population exceeding seventy thousand. Three decades later, in 1890, its residents numbered close to two hundred thousand, making it the largest black city in sub-Saharan Africa. Today Ibadan, with a population of well over a million, remains one of the largest cities on the continent.

As new towns and cities developed in Yorubaland, older ones expanded. But each town tried to become as large and powerful as possible, often destroying the surrounding villages so as to gather larger populations together at one defensive spot.[27] Intense rivalry developed among the Yoruba towns between 1830 and 1855. They desperately searched for a new political system to fill the power vacuum left by the disintegrating Oyo empire. Eventually the town succeeded the kingdom as the effective unit of political organization.[28] Loyalty to town leaders was more essential than allegiance to the sub-cultural groups because only the municipal authorities could ensure one's survival.

Like many Yoruba towns and cities that suddenly blossomed at that time, residence patterns no longer reflected mere kinship ties. Pre-civil war towns such as Old Oyo, Ilorin, and Ife were conglomerations of large family compounds. They were, in effect, a natural outgrowth of the expansion in scale of resident Yoruba families. Indeed, as elsewhere in Africa, early Yoruba towns and villages were visible expressions of lineage and extended-family living patterns. Yet residential conformations in refugee towns of the nineteenth century did not necessarily begin with the kin unit. Instead, particular warriors secured an area within the community and attracted a following of disparate, uprooted groups.

Nineteenth-century Yoruba warfare led to the formation of new towns in western Nigeria. Families fled their farms for the security of the burgeoning war-towns. By contrast, northern Nigeria at the same time was experiencing an urban exodus. This process may be explained by Fulani siege tactics, which forced the Hausa cities to set aside large spaces within their walled confines for food production.

There was an insufficiency of land to feed everyone, and consequently one Hausa city after another capitulated to the Fulani attackers.[29] It became painfully clear that the cities were no longer urban containers but unsafe traps. Thus, many people fled voluntarily and began to build stockades and mud walls around outlying villages. On the Gobir and Zamfara frontiers, the new Sokoto caliphate instituted a military and social policy which provided for the construction of stronghold villages, called *ribats*. It was to these defensive *ribats* that so many non-Hausa peasants were transferred. However, the *ribats* were aimed at securing the northern frontier and preventing the Hausa authorities from re-taking their own cities, which had fallen to the Fulani during the holy war.[30] Throughout the first half of the nineteenth century, some larger cities of the Sokoto caliphate, particularly those near the insecure northern frontier, experienced a considerable loss of population. Clapperton, trekking through northern Nigeria in the 1820s, discovered vast vacant areas within the walled cities of Kano and Katsina. Of the latter city he remarked: "the houses do not occupy above one-tenth the space. . . ."[31] Urbanization declined, but villagization increased dramatically. Nomadic pastoral Fulani were encouraged by their town-oriented Muslim cousins to acquire settled agricultural life-styles more conducive to the practice of Islam. Tent encampments gradually gave way to stable villages with permanent mud and thatch structures.[32]

War, slave raiding, and massive abrupt migrations had similar repercussions in parts of East Africa's interior. Here too they provided a powerful stimulant for the development of town life. For centuries, East African homesites were scattered throughout cultivated fields and gardens. Compact settlements were almost nonexistent. Indeed, the prevailing system of land tenure encouraged isolated dwellings on individual farms. With no foreign threats, there was little need to cluster for survival. However, in the early eighteenth century, the Usumbara of northeastern Tanzania had begun to create towns as a defense against plundering Masai warriors from Kenya.[33] And after 1840, some groups in central Tanzania constructed stone fortress-towns to shield themselves, their farms, and their livestock against Ngoni invaders and avaricious Arab/Swahili slavers. The Hehe leader Mkwana staved off an Ngoni invasion in 1879 by collecting his people into a central palisaded town which became known as Kalenga.

Surrounded by protective stone walls in about 1890, Kalenga became
a temporary bulwark against the German eruptions which followed.[34]

The nineteenth-century conditions of violence, insecurity, and
population movements contributed to the creation of new towns of
administration and defense in southern Africa as well. Imperialistic
South African Zulu wars in the early nineteenth century had originally triggered the Ngoni (Nguni) population movements described
above. Law, order, and security consequently broke down in the
Transvaal and elsewhere. Uncentralized and therefore militarily vul-
nerable grassland societies united in self-defense against warrior bands
fleeing the wrath of Shaka, founder of the Zulu nation. As a result,
some areas of southern Africa experienced considerable urbanization
from the 1820s while others became depopulated. For centuries, the
Transvaal region had contained thousands of towns and villages,
nestled at the base of small chains of conical hills. A total of eighteen
thousand ruins have been estimated in southern Africa, extending
from the Zambesi River to the Orange.[35] Zulu imperialism and its
aftermath destroyed most of these communities. A member of the
London Missionary Society reported this tragic situation on his travels
in the Orange River area in 1829. He noted that at the base of
numerous small mountains and conical hills lay the ruins of innum-
erable towns, "some of amazing extent." The towns gave evidence of
"immense labour and perseverance, every fence being composed of
stones, averaging five or six feet high, raised apparently without
mortar, lime or hammer." The walls of the round houses were so well
plastered and polished that they had the appearance of being var-
nished. He also found that the doors and walls were ornamented with
architraves and cornices.[36]

Not all the communities he encountered lay in desolation. The
larger agglomerations seemed to have survived this period of
Difaqane, or "crushing of peoples" as the Sotho called it. Lattakoo
contained two to three thousand huts with an estimated population of
between ten and fifteen thousand. In circumference it was as large as
Cape Town. Kaditshwene held somewhere around thirteen to sixteen
thousand; and Mashaw town approximately twelve thousand. Some
Rolong peoples were grouped together in towns approaching twenty
thousand.[37]

Nevertheless, open grassland communities in this interior table-land were difficult to defend, and the majority of them ultimately capitulated. Their inhabitants were forced to seek safety on cold, almost inaccessible mountaintops or farther away on the northern plateaux. The rugged Drakensberg range afforded considerable protection. Moshweshwe, father of the Sotho kingdom of Basutoland, collected refugees and established the stronghold of Thaba Bosiu on a great flat-topped hill standing isolated in a fertile plain between the Orange and the Caledon rivers. Its half-square-mile summit provided for the accommodation in times of siege of large numbers of people with livestock and other provisions. Its steep cliffs and narrow passes were excellent natural defenses; and the surrounding countryside could support a substantial population in times of peace.[38] A French missionary spent several decades in Basutoland and described Thaba Bosiu in 1833 as a jumble of low huts, separated only by narrow lanes, crowded with children and dogs. In the town center was a vast space where cattle were penned at night in well-constructed, perfectly round stone enclosures. Adjoining the square was a courtyard devoted to business transactions and public speeches.[39]

In the entire country between the Orange and Limpopo rivers, between the Kalahari desert and the Indian Ocean, only towns blessed with natural defenses were able to withstand the continuous raiding. Considerations of security were paramount in the selection of sites; and because of this criterion, new-town expansion was restricted by limited supplies of water and food.

The confident Zulu, in contrast to this generally unstable condition, constructed many new towns under the supervision of Shaka's well-disciplined warriors. They were ideally situated, well provisioned, and rationally planned. In a typical new town, fourteen hundred domed grass huts were constructed around a circumference of three miles and situated on the side of a hill for purposes of drainage. Structures were evenly spaced and designed so as to retain the privacy of the traditional isolated homestead. Everything fell into a rigid hierarchical pattern. The arrangement of the huts around the circle reflected the autocratic nature of Zulu society.[40]

Shaka's successor and usurper, Dingaan, continued the program of town (kraal) building. Dingaan's greatest achievement in this endeavor was the construction of his massive capital, Umgungundhlovu, in about 1836. Umgungundhlovu was probably the largest

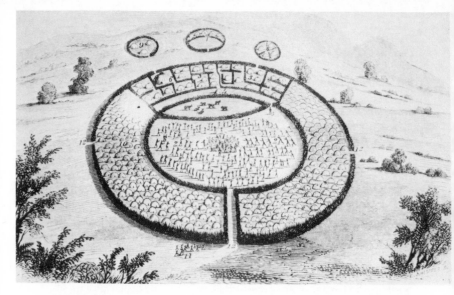

16. Dingaan's royal elliptical kraal at Umgungundhlovu (about 1830). All Zulu royal cities followed a consistent design. These were essentially predatory cities, which thrived not on market or craft activity but on pillage of the surrounding countryside. At its zenith, Umgungundhlovu contained over 1700 dwellings, capable of accommodating twenty soldiers in each. Courtesy Killie Campbell Africana Library.

and most pretentious kraal ever built in southern Africa, comprising well over a thousand beehive dwellings. This grass-made town was easily burned to the ground by Boer commandos in 1838. Zulu kraals were not commercial centers but points of human, bovine, political, and military concentration. Primarily aggressive in intent, they rarely outlived their founders.[41]

Interestingly, comparatively little urban growth occurred in areas lacking centralized institutions of authority and not exposed to external threats or massive infusions of new, culturally dissimilar ethnic groups. The Ibo of eastern Nigeria are an excellent example. Ibo families have lived an urban life for at least three centuries, yet they chose not to construct cities. Disdaining the institution of centralized divine kingship, they had no leaders to whom tribute could be paid. Thus, there was no centralized, bureaucratic authority to command mass labor for the construction of imposing public edifices. Instead, the Ibo lived in loose clusters of homesteads, irregularly scattered along paths which radiated from central meeting places. The Ibo lived in what modern planners would call "cluster communities." Their settlements were separated from each other by sweeping green belts. Thus, while the Ibo were urbanites, they were not city dwellers in the classical sense.[42]

IV.

Many precolonial cities were accidents, beyond the control of the human will. Others were defensive responses to external or internal threats. However, some cities were acts of will, bold attempts to build a new society. Muhammad Bello in 1809, after forging the disparate Hausa city-states into a unified Fulani caliphate, created a new capital city on a bluff overlooking the Sokoto River. Sokoto city overnight became the administrative and religious center of the caliphate bearing its name.[43] Its elegant new mosques were deliberately dispersed throughout the city to facilitate the teaching and practice of Islam by everyone. Sokoto was therefore designed as a thoroughly Islamic city; and its residential architecture was carefully patterned after the mosques. Public squares lined with shade trees stretched before each mosque to enable people to pray communally and comfortably.

Muhammad Bello actively encouraged the founding of new towns, particularly in the western marches of the caliphate. Unlike the Hausa, the Fulani *jihadists* (revolutionaries) and the *mallams* (scholars) were raised in a tradition of shifting pastoralism. They disdained town life and preferred to live in isolated camps beyond the areas of peasant farming and urban dwelling. Bello realized that their life style would have to change if they were to succeed in converting the rural and urban masses to Islam.[44]

Other towns in Africa were created in response to Christian humanitarian opposition to slavery and the slave trade. Beginning in the late eighteenth century, the British established new towns along the West African coast for settlement by freed slaves from England, Jamaica, and Nova Scotia. The Nova Scotians were former American slaves who had fought with the British against the American Revolution in return for promises of emancipation. After the war, they were transported to the cold shores of Nova Scotia. The environment proved not to their liking and about a thousand of them were transferred to Sierra Leone in 1792 to found the community of Freetown. After the abolition of the legal status of the Atlantic slave trade in

1808, they were joined by an increasing flow of liberated Africans who had been taken off illegal slaving vessels and released in Freetown's Vice Admiralty Court. Once converted to Christianity, they were sent into the Sierra Leonean hinterland, along with a few missionaries. Together they established new towns which would serve as "pockets of Western Christian civilization among the savages." These towns were laid out in English style around a nucleus of church and school. Cut off from the cultures of their original homelands, the settlers readily adopted Western life styles and codes of behavior set forth by the missionaries. But the towns themselves were alien to the indigenous population in design and purpose and were looked upon with a mixture of envy and resentment.

The new towns of Liberia, like those in Sierra Leone, were the product of efforts to abolish slavery and the slave trade. They were to serve as model communities which hopefully would be emulated by the *indigenes*. The towns were founded after 1822 by freed black Americans trying to escape the humiliation of racial discrimination in the United States. By the time of Liberian independence in 1847, Monrovia, its capital, had become a town resembling those of the rural American South.

Another settlement of liberated Africans was established in the Gabon estuary in Central Africa by French philanthropists in 1849. It was minuscule and revolved around the new town of Libreville. Not until the late nineteenth century did the French have any pretensions about Libreville serving as a springboard for Western civilization in Africa. Indeed, this Gallic counterpart to Britain's Freetown and America's Monrovia never possessed a sense of mission. Today, Libreville is the booming capital and commercial heart of the independent Republic of Gabon.

V.

The nineteenth century in sub-Saharan Africa was a period of demographic dislocation, social upheaval, and reurbanization. Old cities declined or were destroyed while new ones were born, often in rather rapid and dramatic fashion. But the new urban centers were unlike the old. They were born of strife, and out of the desperate search for a new social, religious, and political order.

In the twentieth century, the European conquerors redesigned these traditional cities to reflect their own conceptions of social, political, and economic organization. In areas exposed to British notions of indirect rule, satellite towns of European administration were constructed just beyond the walls or boundaries of the traditional city. The precolonial cities remained remarkably intact in both layout and architecture. The satellite towns, on the other hand, were often microcosms of the typical English town. In contrast, the French and the Belgians obliterated the traditional cities by superimposing new radial street patterns, similar to Haussmann's nineteenth-century design for Paris. The indigenous populations were removed to *bidonvilles*, or suburbs, of the new towns. Today, modern Dakar, Senegal; or Kinshasa, Zaire, more closely resemble a European city than Ibadan, Nigeria; or Kumasi, Ghana.

[1] S. J. Hogben and A. M. Kirk-Greene, *The Emirates of Northern Nigeria*, (London, 1966), pp. 184–85.

[2] C. C. Ifemesia, "States of the Central Sudan," in J. F. Ade Ajayi and Ian Espie, eds., *A Thousand Years of West African History* (Ibadan, 1967), p. 91.

[3] M. L. Daneel, *The God of the Matopo Hills* (The Hague, 1970), pp. 14–17.

[4] R. C. C. Law, "Traditional History," in S. O. Biobaku, ed., *Sources of Yoruba History* (Oxford, 1973), p. 137.

[5] Robert S. Smith, *Kingdoms of the Yoruba* (London, 1969), p. 11. See also Biobaku, ed., *Sources of Yoruba History*, p. 137.

[6] Emmanuel Effa, "Pedestrians in Kumasi City" (M. S. thesis, Kumasi, 1967).

[7] Kofi Antubam, *Ghana's Heritage of Culture* (Leipzig, 1963), p. 161.

[8] See R. A. Adeleye, *Power and Diplomacy in Northern Nigeria 1804–1906* (New York, 1971), pp. 250–314.

[9] J. M. Gray, "The Kibuga of Buganda," *Uganda Journal* 25, no. 1 (1961): 70.

[10] H. M. Stanley, *Through the Dark Continent* (New York, 1879), 1: 201–2.

[11] H. F. C. Smith, "The Early States of the Central Sudan," in J. F. Ade Ajayi and Michael Crowder, eds., *History of West Africa* (New York, 1972), 1:158–202.

[12] Andrew Roberts, "The Nyamwezi," in Andrew Roberts, ed., *Tanzania before 1900* (Nairobi, 1968), pp. 117–45. See also Norman R. Bennett, *Mirambo of Tanzania c. 1840–1884* (London, 1971).

[13] James B. Wolf, ed., *Missionary to Tanganyika 1877–1888* (London, 1971), p. 66.

[14] Neville Chittick, "Kilwa," in Merrick Posnansky, ed., *Prelude to East African History* (Ibadan, 1966), pp. 125–37.

[15] Ibn Battuta, in G. S. P. Freeman-Grenville, ed. and trans., *East African Coast, Select Documents* (London, 1962), p. 31.

[16] Abdurahman es Sa'di, in Basil Davidson, ed., *The African Past* (New York, 1967), p. 94.

[17] Nehemiah Levtzion, *Ancient Ghana and Mali* (London, 1973), p. 80. See also A. Pardo, "The Songhay under Sonni Ali and Askia Muhammad" in Daniel McCall, ed., *Boston University Papers on Africa* 5 (1971): 23.

[18] Leo Africanus, *History and Description of Africa* (London 1896), 1: 123–28.

[19] T. Edward Bowdich, *Mission from Cape Coast Castle to Ashantee* (London, 1819), p. 323.

[20] Henry Barth, *Travels and Discoveries in North and Central Africa* (New York, 1857), 1: 513–14.

[21] Philip J. C. Dark, *The Introduction to Benin Art and Technology* (Oxford, 1973), pp. 46–53.

[22] D. J. Siddle, "War Towns in Sierra Leone," *Africa* 38, no. 1 (1968): 47–56.

[23] Ivor Wilks, "Ashanti Government," in Daryll Forde and P. M. Kaberry, eds., *West African Kingdoms in the Nineteenth Century* (London, 1967), pp. 229–30.

[24] S. Goddard, "Town-Farm Relationships in Yorubaland," *Africa* 35, no. 1 (1965), 21. See also Eva Krapf-Askari, *Yoruba Towns and Cities* (Oxford, 1969), pp. 52–59.

[25] *Ibid.* pp. 55–56.

[26] Samuel Johnson, *The History of the Yorubas* (London, 1921; reprinted 1969), p. 94. See also R. O. Ekundare, *An Economic History of Nigeria 1860–1960* (New York, 1973), p. 57. For an estimate of Ibadan's population in 1851 see P. C. Lloyd *et al.*, eds., *The City of Ibadan* (Cambridge, 1967), p. 61.

[27] J. F. Ade Ajayi, "The Aftermath of the Fall of Old Oyo," in Ajayi and Crowder, eds., *History of West Africa*, 2:132.

[28] *Ibid.*, p. 136.

[29] Oral Testimony, Mallam Urwatu, Katsina, 23 July 1966.

[30] Murray Last, *The Sokoto Caliphate* (New York, 1967), pp. 74–80.

[31] E. W. Bovill, ed., *Missions to the Niger* (London, 1966), 5:708.

[32] Oral Testimony, Mallam Guda, Katsina, 25 July 1966.

[33] S. Feierman, "The Shambaa," in Roberts, ed., *Tanzania before 1900*, p. 4.

[34] Alison Redmayne, "Mkwana and the Hehe Wars," *Journal of African History* 9, no. 3, (1968), 409–37.

[35] Roger Summers, *Ancient Ruins and Vanished Civilisations of Southern Africa* (Cape Town, 1971), p. 9.

[36] Robert Moffat, *Matabele Journals* (London, 1945), 1:8.

[37] *Ibid.*, p. 8.

[38] J. D. Omer-Cooper, *The Zulu Aftermath* (Evanston, Ill., 1966), p. 101.

[39] Eugene Casalis, in R. C. Germond, ed. and trans., *Chronicles of Basutoland* (Morija, 1967), p. 25.

[40] Barrie Biermann, "Indlu: The Domed Dwelling of the Zulu," in Paul Oliver, ed., *Shelter in Africa* (London, 1971), p. 98.

[41] Killie Campbell, "Umgungundhlovu-Dingaan Kraal" (Durban, n.d.), n.p.

[42] M. M. Green, *Ibo Village Affairs* (1947; 2d edition New York, 1964), p. 21.

[43] Ahmadu Bello, *My Life* (Cambridge, Mass., 1962), p. 12.

[44] Oral Testimony, Mallam Urwatu, Katsina, 16 August 1966.

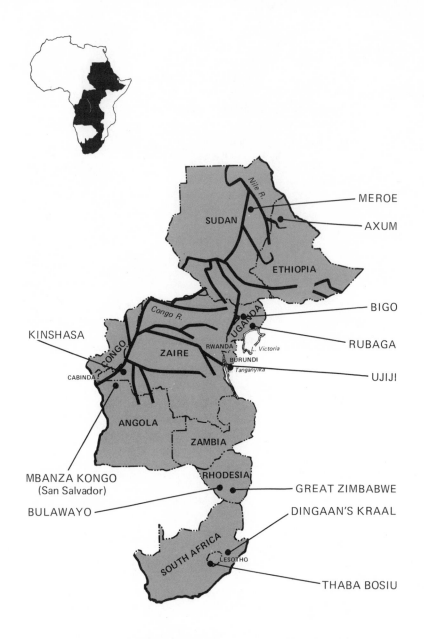

MAJOR CITIES OF EASTERN AND SOUTHERN AFRICA,
591 B.C.—NINETEENTH CENTURY.

MAJOR MEDIEVAL EAST AFRICAN COASTAL CITY-STATES
(WITHIN CONTEXT OF MODERN AFRICA).

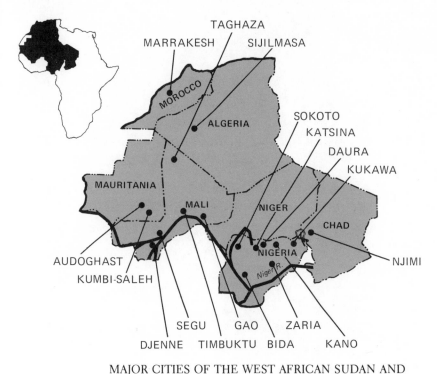

MAJOR CITIES OF THE WEST AFRICAN SUDAN AND
NORTHWEST AFRICA, ELEVENTH–SEVENTEENTH
CENTURIES (WITHIN CONTEXT OF A MAP OF MODERN
AFRICA).

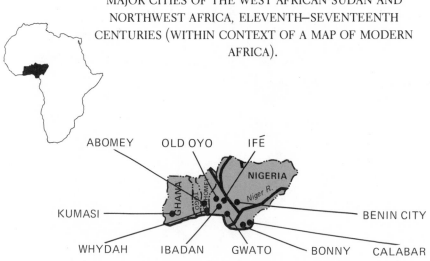

MAJOR CITIES OF WEST AFRICA'S COAST AND HINTERLAND,
NINETEENTH CENTURY.

2
PHYSICAL DEFINITIONS
OF CITIES AND TOWNS

Walls

WALLING was a vitally important consideration in the development of African urban life. Walls gave definition to settlements and prevented uncontrollable urban sprawl. Walls also provided psychic and physical security. In unstable times they afforded protection against theft or destruction. In peacetime they controlled entry and exit.

Politically, walls were considered prestigious, their size a measure of a ruler's ability to command the labor of his or her subjects. In northern Nigeria in the early sixteenth century, Queen Amina of Zaria constructed a high mud wall extending more than a hundred miles. While protecting Hausa markets from external threats emanating in the south, it also became an enduring testimony to the glorious reign of Amina.[1]

African urban walls were also built to overawe foreign visitors. European travelers to Buganda's monarch in the 1860s noted with astonishment that the royal enclosure was encompassed by a twelve-foot-high reed fence made of intricately woven elephant grass and supported by posts made from wild fig trees.[2] Royal compounds everywhere in centralized African states were characterized by a maze of walled galleries and passageways, making it difficult for strangers to reach the final seat of authority. A European visitor to the palace at Benin city in about 1726 reported having to pass first through a "very long gallery" supported by fifty-eight columns. At the end of this passageway he encountered a mud wall containing three gates. Above each gate reposed a large well-cast "copper snake." Passing through the middle gate, he entered a plaza approximately a quarter mile square and surrounded by a low mud wall. From there he was escorted through four more galleries, adorned with metal sculpture which were undoubtedly the now-famous Benin pictorial plaques. Beyond all this lay the king's audience chamber.[3]

Inner walls in African cities protected and defined the royal compound. They maintained the integrity of divine kingship by shielding the monarch from the rude gaze of public scrutiny and preventing the dispersion of state secrets. The techniques of palace craftsmen, the ways of the diviner or medicine man, palace intrigues, and the everyday human activities of the monarch were all kept beyond reach of the urban masses. Inner walls, then, reinforced the mystique of divine kingship. At Ife and Benin, ordinary people were not permitted to witness the almost magical casting of magnificent royal plaques and statues by use of the lost-wax process. Nor in the kingdom of Kanem-Bornu could the public see their Mai, or king, engage in such human activities as eating or sleeping.

In contrast, the outer walls of African cities were the people's walls. Walls shielded the people from foreign attack and allowed merchants to conduct business with confidence. Outer walls also provided the masses with a necessary sense of corporate identity.

Between the inner and outer walls lay scores of secondary ones which defined the parameters of kinship activity and fulfilled the extended families' need for privacy and protection. One could almost view an African city as a series of walled containers, the public ones radiating in concentric circles like ripples on a pond and the private ones filling intervening space like the cellular labyrinth of a beehive.

Numerous gates along urban walls served as effective instruments of economic and population control. At most gates, booths were erected for the collection of tolls on passing goods. Gates were economically important because the tolls collected provided a major source of revenue for the urban government. An eyewitness account of sixteenth century Djenné reveals the existence of eleven city gates.[4]

Nineteenth-century Ibadan possessed four gates, and heart-shaped Katsina boasted of seven. In Hausa cities, each gate was reserved for a specific titled chief and for the people of his own provinces. The

17. The Yoruba city of Ife, indicating the course of the city walls. Courtesy Thames and Hudson, *Ife in the History of West African Sculpture*, Frank Willett, © 1967.

revenue earned by his toll house helped to support his family and personal retainers. In Yoruba towns and cities, tolls levied on all agricultural and marketable commerce were turned over to the city's Oba, or mayor.[5]

Strong architectural emphasis was placed on gates in the Hausa cities. Some of them bore a resemblance to the great fourteenth-century Marinid gateway in Rabat, Morocco, and to the gates of the Andalusian mosque at Fez. The immense gates leading into the cities of Hausaland were made of termite-resistant palm wood covered with iron plates. Breaching them obviously required considerable effort. Only British cannonry in 1902–3 rendered them forever obsolete.

The practice of walling human settlements is of great antiquity. Remains of stone-walled kraal villages in the Transvaal are associated with the Uitkomst and Buispoort cultures, dating between about A.D. 1060 and 1650.[6] Similar though more decorative stone walling is found in the seventeenth-century rainmaking centers of Dhlo-Dhlo, Naletali, and Khami. Their decorative patterns and mode of construction more closely resemble those at Great Zimbabwe.

From at least the fourteenth century, defense-minded residents of Great Zimbabwe created thirty-two-foot-high elliptical walls of carefully cut stone, which they laid in herringbone, chevron, cord, and checkerboard patterns. The outer wall of the Great Enclosure contains some 182,000 cubic feet of stonework and is over eight hundred feet long. The Great Enclosure is by far the largest single prehistoric structure in sub-Saharan Africa.[7]

The "Zimbabwe technique" was practiced over a wide area, extending far south of the Limpopo River. Indeed, there seem to be striking

18. Remains of one of the major gateways in the Hausa city of Katsina in northern Nigeria. The great outer wall of Katsina was built by Sarki (king) Ali Murabus (d. 1568/9). Author's photo.

19. Gateway to a medieval city in the Sultanate of Morocco. Morocco was a major trading partner of the Western Sudanic cities and made a significant architectural impact. Photo: Martha Horsley.

technical similarities and continuities between the Venda stone walls in South Africa and those north of the Limpopo on the Rhodesian plateau. However, the walling at Great Zimbabwe probably represents the most elaborate stage of development, possible because of the city's great wealth and realized because of its desire for ostentation. Equally important, at Great Zimbabwe and vicinity, rocks could easily be broken into slabs by heating the surface and then cooling it rapidly with cool water.[8] Unlike most stone-walling, the early walls at Great Zimbabwe were extensions of enormous natural boulders.

The main body of stone builders in the South African Transvaal may have been the Sotho peoples. Unlike their neighbors, they lived in large settlements rather than on scattered homesites.[9] Their stone-building techniques spread widely. The walls of the Great Enclosure at Great Zimbabwe may have been build by the Sotho peoples under coercion from their overlords in the Mwenemutapan empire.[10]

Zimbabwe, a word believed to be of Shona origin, means "structures of stone"; and there are indeed many zimbabwes scattered

20. Decorative mortarless stone walling at Dhlo Dhlo (in Rhodesia). Apparently built by the Rozvi-Shona in the seventeenth and eighteenth centuries. Author's photo.

21. Passageway to the hill ruin at Great Zimbabwe. Author's photo.

22. Steps leading into the Great Enclosure at Great Zimbabwe. The walls and entrance were constructed in about 1440–50, without the use of mortar or any other adhering compound. Author's photo.

23. Double walling and a narrow waving passageway. The Great Enclosure at Great Zimbabwe. Author's photo.

throughout southern Africa, from the Rhodesian plateau down through the northern Transvaal. Great Zimbabwe may have been the most impressive, but there were others of considerable size. In 1552 a Portuguese compiler described at second hand the stone-walled city of Matendere, some one hundred miles northeast of Great Zimbabwe:

> in the midst of the plain there is a square fortress, of masonry within and without, built of stones of marvellous size, and there appears to be no mortar joining them. The wall is more than twenty-five spans in width. . . . The edifice is almost surrounded by hills, upon which are others resembling it in the fashioning of the stone and the absence of mortar and one of them is a tower more than twelve fathoms high.[11]

The stone-construction techniques of southern Africa are somewhat similar to those of East Africa. Stone-foundationed village ruins on Hyrax Hill above Lake Nakuru in Kenya's highlands have been dated to the Neolithic period and are quite similar to those in the post-eleventh century A.D. Transvaal. Does this similarity imply a stone-building tradition extending from the interlacustrine region of East Africa to the South African grasslands? This tantalizing question awaits an answer.

The practice of surrounding settlements with walls is also found in early West Africa. The word *birane* has been used since at least the twelfth century A.D. to describe the walled settlements of the Hausa peoples of northern Nigeria. The emergence of Hausa walled towns may be associated with the introduction of iron technology, which allowed for greater agricultural surpluses, and the arrival of desert immigrants in the early part of the first millennium A.D. These towns provided surrounding farms with industrial goods, such as iron implements, and in turn absorbed agricultural produce.[12] Unlike the earlier hamlets, the *biranes* contained a diversity of peoples lacking bonds of common origin or kinship. The walls were primarily defensive in intent, to shield the inhabitants from external attacks and to protect such vital industries as iron smelting. The walls were gradually expanded over the centuries as towns grew into cities and as they became more exposed to prolonged sieges. Ultimately, a second wall would be built to enclose an area for food production during siege periods. Such outer walls sometimes acquired monumental dimensions. For example, the outer wall of Kano city in the late nineteenth century was twenty feet wide at the base, thirty feet high, and had a circumference of twelve miles, enclosing an area of sixteen square miles.[13] The first set of walls in Kano were begun by Sarki (king) Gijinmasu (*ca.* 1095–1134) and completed by his son in about 1150.[14]

The walled cities we have examined so far were located in relatively open and exposed grasslands. However, walls also surrounded forest communities. In about 1440 Eware the Great, ruler of the Benin kingdom, constructed high walls and deep protective trenches around Benin city.[15] A European visitor about 1660 noted:

> The town, comprising the queen's court, is about five or six miles in circumference. . . . It is protected at one side by a wall ten feet high, made of double stockades of big trees, tied to each other by cross-beams fastened cross-wise, and stuffed up with red clay, solidly put together. This wall only surrounds the town on one side, there being on the other, where there is no wall, a morass and close underwood, which affords no little protection and strength to the town. The town possesses several gates, eight or nine feet in height and five in width, with doors made of a whole piece of wood, hanging or turning on a peg. . . .[16]

After the fifteenth century, Yoruba towns had also begun to acquire walls. However, it was not until the late nineteenth century, after constant civil war, that a Yoruba clergyman could state that every town was walled and surrounded by deep trenches. Smaller towns further fortified themselves by encouraging thickets to grow approximately one-half to one mile from the community walls.[17]

But not all African towns and cities considered walls essential. To settlements defined and protected by natural features, walls seemed unnecessary. Some cities found that moats or deep trenches would suffice. A Portuguese mariner who visited the port city of Gwato in the Benin kingdom wrote in 1550 that it had "no wall but is surrounded by a large moat, very wide and deep, which suffices for its defense."[18] Residents of Kumasi, living on a hill surrounded by marshy, almost impenetrable land, also found wall construction unnecessary. Townsmen in sixteenth-century Kongo, whose dwellings customarily lay in defensive positions far off the major paths, made the same decision. Public walling was also absent on the East African coast, where city-states were either separated from the mainland by channels of water or rested on spits of land.

Passageways

Passageways are the most basic units of public space; and African towns and cities displayed an exceptional understanding of the need for such human conveyors. Dwellings were constructed exceedingly close to each other, but blocks of buildings were separated by narrow alleys. Many of the larger towns and cities were intersected by avenues, and alleyways not only opened onto these broad thoroughfares but were broken by pleasant community plazas. In politically centralized societies, particularly Asante, Yoruba, Hausa, and Ganda, towns tended to be radial concentric with roads commencing at the royal compound or central marketplace and radiating to the various provincial centers. Normally, each chief assumed responsibility for maintaining the paths that extended to his own provincial seat.

The practice of intersecting towns with a single great broad avenue is of considerable antiquity. Kumbi-Saleh's main thoroughfare in the eleventh century was thirty-nine feet wide.[19] Akan towns in the Asante Confederacy were characterized by a major long avenue with a north-south orientation. Side streets joined the avenue at near right angles. In Kumasi, all avenues had names, and four of the main passageways had widths of between fifty and a hundred yards.[20] Roads in the kingdom of Buganda were equally impressive. Stanley, who visited Buganda's capital in 1875, was struck by the road network which comprised "very broad avenues, imperial enough in width." He added that "each avenue was fenced with tall matete (water cane) neatly set very close together in uniform rows." Passageways leading from one avenue to another were narrow and crooked.[21]

Broad ceremonial avenues were also observed by a Dutchman in Benin city in 1602. Some six decades later, another European writer said, "The town has thirty very straight and broad streets, every one of them about one hundred and twenty feet wide. . . ."[22] Like Buganda's capital, narrow passageways intersected the avenues at right angles. Both cities in precolonial Africa exhibited a gridiron pattern. Others had modified grids. Abbé Proyart's description of Loango city in Central Africa in about 1770 hints at a grid layout; and Heinrich Barth in the nineteenth century described Timbuktu as laid out partly in rectangular fashion.[23] Gridiron street lay-outs, radial concentric passageways and broad ceremonial avenues were not uncommon under conditions of extreme centralization of power. Monarchs needed such avenues to receive massive processions of chiefly delegations from outlying provinces. In Kumasi and elsewhere, they were grand pedestrian ways, with market stalls or the houses of important dignitaries along the curbs.

The Intimacy of Urban Space

Nearly all human habitations in Africa possessed a certain sacred quality. The land beneath them belonged not to the living but to the dead, the ancestors. And the cities themselves were an integral part of the life process. Their various quarters were as sacred as life itself and could not be disturbed unless the proper spiritual forces had been consulted. It is therefore not surprising that Africans sought to define the physical parameters of their habitations.

African society remained essentially agrarian, and urbanites never completely lost their roots in the earth. Thus, even in town there was a sense of the country. Animals wandered at will, there was an abundance of space, buildings seldom soared more than a story high, and ornamental trees often shaded the main streets, avenues, and plazas.

24. View of Benin city in 1891 before the British conquest. Note the gridiron street pattern. H. Ling Roth, *Great Benin*, Barnes and Noble reprint, 1968.

25. Precolonial brass box and a peaque, both representing the high-pitched shingled roof turrets of an important palace. Such structures were described by a European visitor in 1787. H. Ling Roth, *Great Benin*, Barnes and Noble reprint, 1968.

26. View of Utiri village in Central Africa. Observe the alignment of rectangular dwellings along a straight roadway (late nineteenth century, before the European conquest). Henry M. Stanley, *Through the Dark Continent*, Vol. I, Harper Brothers, 1879.

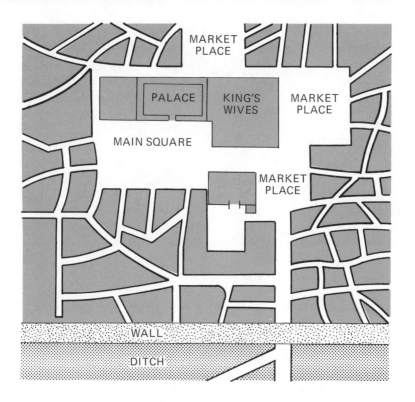

Towns in a sense were overgrown rural villages, the major differences
being in scale of population, extent of market activity, or the proportion of people engaged in specialized occupations.

Community layouts mirrored the laws of nature and the forces of
philosophical thought. So humane were African towns and cities that
they were regarded by their inhabitants as concrete expressions of their
inner thoughts about man, nature, and the cosmos. Like all living
organisms, component parts never lost their interrelatedness. Each
activity was situated in an area of optimum benefit to the corporate
body. As a human heart is located within proximity to the most vital
organs of the body, a chief's compound stood near the shrine, market,
or women's huts. Some settlements were even anthropomorphic in
design—being representations of their human occupants. Dogon
farmers, living on cliffs south of the Niger's waters, offer a striking

27. A typical community well, focus of social interaction in the ancient northern Nigerian city of Katsina. Author's photo.

illustration. Their deeply spiritual communities symbolized the human body, reposing in a north-south direction. Villagers likened the blacksmith's forge to a head, the community shrines to feet, and the women's menstrual huts to the hands.[24]

The rural character of towns was enhanced by a remarkably efficient use of space within enclosed communities. Yao townsmen of east central Africa came to terms with urban living by cultivating every square plot of open land. Even cassava, a staple food, sprouted along heavily trodden paths.[25] Northward in the royal capital of Buganda, banana gardens surrounded each dwelling. They lent a serene impression of rural spaciousness, yet provided an essential ingredient to the urbanite's diet.

Africans were adept at maintaining that feeling of smallness and rural intimacy, even in areas of high population density. In eighteenth-century Mbanza Kongo, houses were widely spaced and encompassed by lush green grasses and palisades of tall leafy trees. Just to the north lay a magnificent sylvan retreat where men were forbidden to remove trees or to disrupt in any way the ecological balance.[26] Nearby, the Bashilele built their houses around existing trees. Since it was a criminal offense to cut down a raphia or an oil palm tree, builders had to accommodate themselves to the natural order of things.[27] In northern Zaire (Congo), Bangala towns were built around a large square which had to be bordered by rectangular patches of banana plants and double rows of palm trees, laid out in a straight line.[28]

Ibo peoples of eastern Nigeria were perhaps the most successful of all at achieving a sense of smallness. As astonishingly efficient use of space was obtained by establishing a cluster plan of development. In Iboland there were no towns or cities, only hundreds of villages separated by large open spaces and groves of shady trees. A series of wooded paths led from the clusters of family compounds to a central meeting place. From these, a wider path continued to a still larger gathering point, serving simultaneously numerous extended families. At that location, another path would snake its way to a market-place, utilized by several wards or extended family clusters.[29]

In oval-shaped towns and cities of the western and central Sudan, green belts separated residential areas from massive mud palisades. These delightful verdant corridors were not purely for esthetic purposes. Farms and orchards flourished on them and supported the towns and cities in time of siege or famine. Like the Ibo pattern, they too imparted a refreshing sense of rurality within an area of high human density.

IGBO (IBO) VILLAGES.

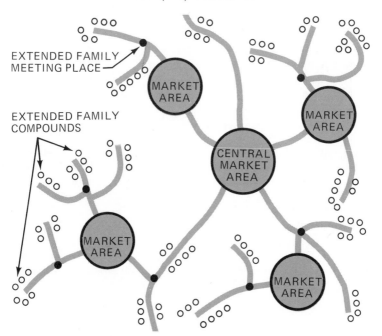

In conclusion, it may be suggested that precolonial African towns and cities minimized urbanism and the feeling of congestion while making maximum use of urban space. Small open spaces (plazas, public wells, and washing areas) were dispersed throughout the city. Large spaces appeared on the periphery (vegetable gardens) and at the center near the palace (parade ground, market). Nearly everywhere, urban development was concentrated, despite low densities. Sudanic and Swahili city layouts in particular reveal patterns of tight compound clustering. Such spatial intimacy lent a feeling of cohesiveness. Yet because of the delicate balance of mass and space, traditional towns and cities were able to achieve a vital neutrality between urban and rural.

[1] Philip N. Logan, "The Walled City of Kano," *Journal of British Architects* 36, no. 10, (1929), 402–6. Also S. J. Hogben and A. M. Kirk-Greene, *The Emirates of Northern Nigeria* (London, 1966), pp. 216–18.

[2] Richard Stanley and Alan Neame, eds., *The Exploration Diaries of H. M. Stanley* (London, 1961), p. 107. Also J. Roscoe, *The Buganda* (London, 1911), p. 368.

[3] Basil Davidson, ed., *The African Past* (New York, 1964), p. 224.

[4] *Ibid.*, p. 94; Raymond Mauny, *Tableau géographique de l'ouest africain au Moyen Age* (Dakar, 1961), p. 500.

[5] G. J. A. Ojo, *Yoruba Palaces* (London, 1966), p. 22.

[6] R. R. Inskeep, "The Archaeological Background," in Monica Wilson and L. M. Thompson, eds., *The Oxford History of South Africa*, (Oxford, 1969), 1:35.

[7] Peter S. Garlake, *Great Zimbabwe* (London, 1973), p. 27.

[8] Roger Summers, *Ancient Ruins and Vanished Civilisations of Southern Africa* (Cape Town, 1971), 5:147.

[9] M. Wilson, "The Nguni People," in Wilson and Thompson, eds., *Oxford History of South Africa*, p. 112. In 1801 the town of Lattakoo had a population of ten to fifteen thousand. In 1820, Kaditshwene contained some thirteen to sixteen thousand, and Mashaw, ten to twelve thousand. *Ibid.*, p. 153.

[10] James Walton, *African Village* (Pretoria, 1956), p. 72.

[11] Summers, *Ancient Ruins*, 5:48–49.

[12] Abdullahi Smith in: J. F. Ade Ajayi and Michael Crowder, eds., *History of West Africa* (New York, 1972), 1:186.

[13] C. K. Meek, *The Northern Tribes of Nigeria* (London, 1925), p. 33; W. B. Morgan and J. C. Pugh, *West Africa* (London, 1969), p. 54.

[14] H. R. Palmer, *Sudanese Memoirs* (London, 1918), 3:100–1.

[15] Aku Omokhodion, "The Bini Culture" (M. S. thesis, Kumasi, 1967).

[16] H. Ling Roth, *Great Benin* (1903; reprinted New York, 1968), p. 160.

[17] Samuel Johnson, *The History of the Yorubas* (London, 1921; reprinted 1969), p. 91.

[18] Adu Boahen, ed., *Horizon History of Africa* (New York, 1971), p. 191.

[19] Nehemiah Levtzion, *Ancient Ghana and Mali* (London, 1973), p. 24.

[20] See Emmanuel Effah, "Pedestrians in Kumasi City" (M. S. thesis, Kumasi, 1967), p. 37; T. Edward Bowdich, *Mission from Cape Coast Castle to Ashantee* (London, 1819), pp. 304–14. Governor Winniett visited Kumasi in 1848 and observed, "Kumasi is very different in its appearance from any other native town I have seen in this part of Africa. The streets are generally very broad and clean, and ornamented with many beautiful banana trees, affording . . . shade. . . ." See Freda Wolfson, ed., *Pageant of Ghana* (London, 1958), pp. 124–25.

[21] John Alan Rowe, "Revolution in Buganda," (Ph.D. diss., U. of Wisconsin, 1966), pp. 13–16; Stanley and Neame, eds., *Diaries of Stanley*, p. 73. Roscoe reports that each chief had to maintain in good order a road some forty yards wide from the capital to his county seat (see Roscoe, *Buganda*, p. 62).

[22] Roth, *Great Benin*, p. 160.

[23] Abbe Proyart, *History of Loango* (London, 1776), p. 561. Houses could be readily bought in the marketplace.

[24] M. Griaule and G. Dieterlen, "The Dogon," in Daryll Forde, ed., *African Worlds* (London, 1968), pp. 83–111.

[25] Personal field notes, Dar es Salaam, 11 August 1970.

[26] Georges Balandier, *Daily Life in the Kingdom of the Kongo* (New York, 1968), p. 88.

[27] Harry Johnston, *George Grenfell and the Congo* (New York, 1969), 2:742.

[28] *Ibid.*, 2: 751. Vansina notes that houses in the Tio kingdom of the Middle Congo in the late nineteenth century had roofs of ogival or semicircular form. From afar, they resembled covered wagons drawn up together around the courtyard like spokes of a wheel (see Jan Vansina, *The Tio Kingdom of the Middle Congo, 1880–1892* (London, 1973), p. 155.

[29] It would appear that Nupe villages were laid out in similar fashion. Each cluster formed an *Efu* or ward. *Efus* were separated by stretches of open land containing cultivated fields. See S. F. Nadel, *A Black Byzantium* (London, 1942; 2d edition Oxford, 1961), p. 35. In Uganda, the Gisu displayed a similar living pattern. Male inhabitants of a village cluster were usually members of a common lineage. Villages, consisting of several neighborhoods, were grouped to form village-clusters. See J. S. La Fontaine, "The Gisu of Uganda," in *Ethnographic Survey of Africa* (London, 1959), 10:30.

3

ORIGINS AND EVOLUTION OF AFRICAN HABITATIONS

Sub-Saharan African towns and cities in the precolonial era exhibited a considerable diversity of habitations, some circular, others square or rectangular. The massive reed palaces in the capitals of Buganda and Bunyoro in East Africa were conical in form and often soared more than twenty feet into the air from a base thirty feet in diameter. Their design, reputedly of great antiquity, may have been introduced by pre-thirteenth-century pastoralists who migrated southward from the west bank of the upper Nile. In some respects their royal structures resembled the onion-shaped flat bamboo dwellings of the Sidamo in Ethiopia. The similarity suggests that many centuries ago, before their migrations, the two groups were in contact with each other.

Grassland dwellings of South Africa, in contrast, were lower, more hemispherical and frequently beehive-like in form. Early European travelers described the frameworks of the Cape and Natal Nguni, the Khoi and the Swazi huts as a series of semicircular arches, crossed at right angles by another series of similar arches. James Walton has expressed the belief that the forms had ". . . been developed from a shelter such as that made by the bushmen and more particularly the Congo Pygmies."[1] No one knows for sure, but they undoubtedly predate the Iron Age Bantu migrations into South Africa. Dwellings of the Xhosa, Sotho, and Tembu are more rounded, with a circle of bent

28. Beehive dome dwellings in South Africa. Author's photo.

saplings joined at the apex and strengthened by a series of concentric hoops, parallel to the ground.

Similar structures, though bell-shaped, existed among such disparate seminomadic groups as the Fipa of Tanzania and the early Kanembu in the Lake Chad region. These simple little huts were made of straw loosely bound together. Like the conical and beehive forms, they required little time and energy to build.

The most widespread and prevalent form of habitation south of the Sahara was the cone-on-cylinder. These more permanent structures were preferred by sedentary agriculturalists and town-dwellers. Cone-on-cylinders flourished from the Senegal region eastward across the dry grasslands to Cameroon; in the savannas of Angola and Zaire; throughout most of Tanzania; in Zambia, Malawi, Mozambique; and in Rhodesia and South Africa.

Initially, cylinders were made either with an interwoven twig framework impregnated with mud for support, or by a series of poles with mud pressed in between them. However, since at least the mid-thirteenth century some Africans had begun to discover that walls could be built entirely of earth without a wooden superstructure. Pole-and-mud cylinders nonetheless predominated, particularly in scattered sections of eastern and southern Africa. In the West African savanna, the most common pre-Islamic form was the thatched cone upon a wholly mud or woven-thatch cylinder.

29. Bread-loaf–shaped dwelling in South Africa (Zulu). Women were mainly responsible for construction, including weaving and plaiting the grass covering. Author's photo.

30. Onion-textured dwelling, common in southern Africa's Transvaal and among the Sidamo in Ethiopia. Author's photo.

31. Inverted cone thatched dwelling, built by the Chagga in the foothills of Mount Kilimanjaro. Note how well it blends into the surrounding natural undergrowth. This conical form is similar to the precolonial dwellings of Ganda aristocrats in the Kingdom of Buganda. Author's photo.

32. Musgu clay dwelling (Lake Chad area) shaped like the tip of a bullet, or an egg. The structure is built like a vase and is the work of potters, not masons. Henry M. Stanley, *Through the Dark Continent*, Vol. I, Harper Brothers, 1879.

33. Serombo dwellings in the East African hinterland. The king's palace on the right was thirty feet high and fifty-four feet in diameter. The walls were made of interwoven poles, plastered over with mud (1876). Henry M. Stanley, *Through the Dark Continent*, Vol. 1, Harper Brothers, 1879.

34. Bell-shaped Fipa dwelling in Tanzania. Author's photo.

Still persistent is the misconception that precolonial Africans lived almost exclusively in circular mud and thatch dwellings. Illustrated popular magazines since the mid-nineteenth century have associated most traditional Africans with round, thatched-roof mud-walled huts. However, historical research indicates that square and rectangular forms are of great antiquity and have existed in diverse geographical regions. Undoubtedly, some of the structures were influenced by external architectural traditions. During Rome's occupation of North Africa the rectangular house with an atrium or open inner courtyard became a popular aristocratic style. The conception may later have filtered into Morocco and from there to her trading partners across the desert in the western Sudan.

In East Africa, the growth of Swahili civilization along the coast was accompanied by buildings strikingly similar to those in southern Arabia. Yet in some interior regions, especially where rainfall was light and thatch scarce, flat-roofed rectangular buildings antedated alien cultural contact. Habitations of the Hehe and Gogo of Tanzania and of the Masai reveal rectilinear characteristics totally unlike coastal structures. The same may be said for the dwellings of the Sebei, who since precolonial times have built long, low, rectangular houses on the southern slopes of Mount Elgon in Uganda.[2]

Archeological evidence has revealed that West Africans living not far from the Gold Coast in modern Ghana built rectangular structures long before the great age of European discovery that commenced in the fifteenth century. Indeed, there are impressive thirteenth-century ruins of rectangular structures with clay-built rooms enclosing a stone-paved patio. Also, an Iron Age village of flat-roofed rectangular structures flourished on an escarpment overlooking the White Volta River.[3] Some historians believe that the ancestors of modern

35. Bakikundi dwelling (Uganda, base of Ruwenzori mountains) 1889. The doorways of these structures were elaborately ornamented with triangles painted red and black. Henry M. Stanley, *Through the Dark Continent*, Vol. I, Harper Brothers, 1879.

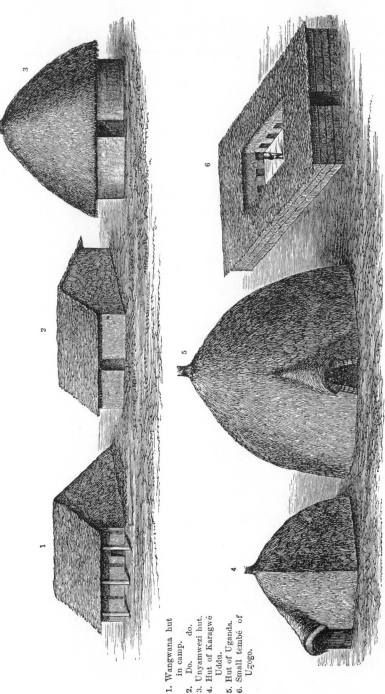

1. Wangwana hut in camp.
2. Do.   do.
3. Unyamwezi hut.
4. Hut of Karagwé Uddu.
5. Hut of Uganda.
6. Small tembé of Ugogo.

36. Different dwelling styles in East Africa's hinterland in the late nineteenth century. Henry M. Stanley, *Through the Dark Continent*, Vol. I, Harper Brothers, 1879.

37. Dwellings at Mtuyu in the Luama valley, 1876. Henry M. Stanley, *Through the Dark Continent*, Vol. I, Harper Brothers, 1879.

Ghanaians came from the Sahara and its southern fringes. Had they been in contact with Romans from North Africa, and did they frequent their cities? If not, did the style of their buildings evolve autonomously? These questions still beg answers. More conclusive, however, is the later proliferation in the western Sudan of Muslim-inspired rectangular forms. But those forms were quite different from those in what is now Ghana.

In East Africa's interior, rectangular forms did not become common until the nineteenth century. They became more apparent as commercial contacts increased between coast and interior, particularly among groups most deeply involved in long-distance trade. Swahili-type structures had appeared in northeastern Tanzania at the outset of the nineteenth century.[4] By the 1860s the Nyamwezi (active long-distance traders to the coast) had begun to construct rectangular houses reflecting dwelling designs of the eastern Congo and the coast, both areas serving as the Nyamwezi's extreme points of trade.[5] On the shores of Lake Tanganyika, especially at Ujiji, Arab-Swahili traders by 1860 had constructed rectangular warehouses with sweeping verandahs.[6] Ujiji became a kind of architectural crossroads. Joseph Thomson in 1881 wrote that the houses "represented almost every style of African architecture—the huge-roofed Indian bungalow, the flat-roofed Tembe, the quadrangular huts of the Waswahili with baraza in front, and the beehived-shaped hut of most of the natives, with composite forms of every description."[7] In the interlacustrine kingdoms northwest of Lake Victoria, rectangular houses were being built after 1885 by retired Nubian soldiers formerly under Emin Pasha.[8]

Southwestward in the central Congo basin, rectangular building forms were evolving long before Arab and European conquests and colonization. For centuries, long, low, rectangular houses were con-

38. Nyamwezi pole and mud thatched dwelling (Tanzania). Author's photo.

39. Nyakyusa lashed-pole dwelling (Tanzania). Author's photo.

40. Pole and mud dwelling (Rhodesia-Ndebele). Poles are set in a raised mud foundation. Mud is pressed between each pole and roof is laid in tiers. These dwellings were common to the area around Great Zimbabwe. Author's photo.

41. Construction of a Venda dwelling (South Africa). Sun-dried mud bricks are laid in place and then plastered over with a fine mixture of clay. Author's photo.

42. Bulk mud thatched dwelling (Dagomba, Ghana). Entrance is decorated with shards of porcelain dishes pressed into the facade. Roof is neatly thatched in tiers. Author's photo.

structed in continuous rows along long, broad thoroughfares. The average Bangala dwelling in the Congo's Equator district extended for twenty-four feet with a breadth of seven and a half feet and a height of five feet ten inches under the roof ridge.[9] A few ethnic groups in central Congo (now Zaire) lived in square houses, supporting sharply vertical roofs. The roofs of Panga dwellings rose like a four-sided cone, some reaching a height of eighteen feet.[10] Bakuba and Bashongo royal houses were also steeple-crowned and pyramidal, though seldom over twelve to fourteen feet high.[11] The origin of this form is unknown. However, the buildings resemble square houses with pyramidal roofs

43. Classical Venda cone-on-cylinder structure with white-washed painted and designed walls. Author's photo.

44. Cone-on-cylinder stone Sotho dwellings, common to Moshweshwe's southern African Kingdom of Basutoland in the nineteenth century. Note that the area around the entrance is smoothly plastered over for esthetic effect. Author's photo.

45. Construction of conical roof superstructure (Venda, South Africa). Author's photo.

found among the Bamileke peoples in Cameroon. Some historians have postulated a distinct architectural tradition extending from central Zaire into the Cameroon highlands.

Rectangular forms had begun to penetrate towns and cities of the West African Sudan at an early period, long before the European conquest. The medieval town mosques of the western and central Sudan bear a likeness (in portals and minaret) to the great ninth-century mosque at Kairouan in Tunisia and to similar structures in the cities of early Morocco. [12] Tower mosques in North Africa had first appeared in eleventh-century Ghardaia (Algeria), when they were constructed by the Ibadites, Islamic fundamentalists who fled Iraq two centuries earlier. [13] Could these mosques have been prototypes? The question awaits an answer. We do know that by the eleventh century, Ghana's capital at Kumbi-Saleh contained several Moorish-style buildings—most of them in cut stone. And in the early thirteenth century Mai (king) Salma of Kanem built clay-boxed mosques. [14]

The rectangular box of clay with a flat roof undoubtedly became a more common form after about 1325. At that time, Mansa Musa of Mali returned from his pilgrimage to Mecca with Abu Ishaq as-Sahili, a Spanish architect who purportedly introduced mud-brick architecture to the western Sudan. [15] As-Sahili's burnt-brick structural schemes (*e.g.*, Sankoré mosque) easily blended into the already-prevailing Djenné mosque forms which since the twelfth century had resembled massive anthills of the locality.

The conversion of Sudanic monarchs to Islam and their growing awareness of Middle Eastern and North African forms strongly influenced architectural styles in West Africa's grasslands. Malekite law insisted on a square or rectangular Friday mosque; and Sudanic monarchs made every effort to construct their palaces in the idiom of the mosque. It became prestigeous to live and worship in structures

46. Construction of an Asante pole wall framework (Ghana). Laterite clay will be pressed into the framing and roof will be thatched with local grasses. Author's photo.

47. Thatching a twig superstructure (East African coast, Kenya). Author's photo.

48. Nyakyusa dwelling. Poles lashed together without the use of mud. Note projecting roof which rests on a large ridge pole (Tanzania). Author's photo.

49. Flat, low mud-roofed pole and mud dwelling built by the Gogo (Tanzania). The mud walls are often more than ten inches thick and the thatched roof is daubed with earth. This structure is the typical rectangular *tembe* found throughout central Tanzania. Author's photo.

50. Earthen walls, mud hump-roofed dwelling with open interior courtyard. Built by the He-he of Tanzania. Author's photo.

51. Bulk mud, aerodynamically shaped windowless Masai dwelling (Tanzania). Constructed of branches plastered with mud and cow dung. Author's photo.

52. High square-box under pyramidal roof. Built by the Dogon (Mali).
Courtesy Carole Howard.

53. Rectangular mud and finely thatched dwelling set neatly in a coconut
grove on Zanzibar Island. Zaramo people (Tanzania). Author's photo.

mirroring those of the Holy Land. Thus, from the fourteenth century,
centers such as Timbuktu, Djenné, and Gao took on the appearance
of Middle Eastern and North African cities. However, the architectural style was unique in that, without stone or long timbers, buildings
had to be constructed with mud bricks and short wooden branches

gathered from local scrubland. These materials dictated a pyramidal verticality and an extensive wooden superstructure. The exterior walls exhibited a prickly effect as the small wooden sticks protruded from the mud surface.

Later, the Timbuktu/Djenné mosque style radiated southeastward. It was carried into the high grasslands of modern Ghana and the Ivory Coast by Muslim Dyula traders and into Hausaland by scholars and merchants fleeing the Moroccan invaders of Songhay. In the Hausa cities, they merged with styles brought down by Tunisian Muslim scholars who settled in Kano around 1534 after the Ottoman occupation of Tunis.[16]

The evolution of Sudanic architecture had been greatly accelerated by the introduction of burnt-brick wall construction. It led to a dramatic move away from walls made of weaker thatch, reinforced earth, or wattle-and daub. Burnt bricks (sun dried in the western Sudan, kiln dried in the central Sudan) made it easier to construct rectangular buildings with stronger, more durable walls that permitted multistory construction. The walls of mosques and chiefly homes could now support heavy flat clay roofs and even domes. The importa-

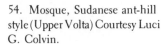

54. Mosque, Sudanese ant-hill style (Upper Volta) Courtesy Luci G. Colvin.

55. Gobiran Mosque, Katsina City (northern Nigeria). This mosque was built in the fifteenth century, when the Hausa kingdoms shared strong cultural and economic ties with Songhay. It is constructed of mud mixed with a vegetable matter (katse) and oxen blood. Author's photo.

56. Interior of the audience chamber of the Naba (king) of Karaga. Karaga, on the forest fringe of West Africa, was a great city of the late–nineteenth-century Mandinka empire of Samory Toure. Note the wall murals, depicting cavalrymen and warriors marching into battle (1880s). L. G. Binger, *Voyage du Niger au Golfe de Guinée*, Paris, 1888.

57. The dwelling of a Sudanic Fulani paramount chief (Katsina Emirate, northern Nigeria). This is typical of the clay box-on-dome structures. Note the sloping walls which draw the eye upward to the delicate spires at the corners. Walls are plastered and white-washed. Author's photo.

tion of termite-resistant palm timbers into northern Nigeria enabled the Hausa to construct domes and clay roofs of almost monumental dimensions. Initially, the domes were supported by a central pillar. But between 1469 and 1499 prosperity came to Kano and imported timber arches were now doubled, allowing for the removal of the central pillar. Domes of an extraordinary symmetry were constructed, despite the fact that builders possessed no rule, level, plumb, or blueprints. These structures, with their high vaulted ceilings, imparted an exhilarating sense of inner space. Outside, an area surrounding the dome was defined by delicate spires at the four corners of the building. Hugh Clapperton, visiting Sokoto city in the early nineteenth century, marveled at the Sultan's new domical residence. It contained

> a square tower, the ceiling of which was a dome, supported by eight ornamental arches, with a bright plate of brass in its center. Between the arches and the outer wall of the tower, the dome was encircled by a neat balustrade in front of a gallery, which led into an upper suite of rooms. [17]

Sudanic architecture did not penetrate the humid forests to any degree because the flat-roofed clay structures could not withstand heavy and prolonged rainfall. In the dry grasslands, a clay roof enjoys the distinct advantage of being fireproof.

The origins of rectangular structures in the rain forests of West Africa remain shrouded in mystery. In the forests of what are today Ghana and Nigeria the most common form consisted of a large four-unit building with verandahs and surrounding an open square courtyard. It was clearly a negative adaptation to an area of heavy rainfall, for water must be drawn out of the sunken courtyard. The rectangular shape and roof of each of the four units was structurally similar to that of the ridge-pole forest dwellings, which were found from Rio del Rey to Benguela in Angola. However, the sunken courtyard, or impluvium, must have been introduced from the north. Although Dyula traders may have brought the Sankoré/Djenné mosque style into the Volta basin; oral traditions suggest that the impluvium form was carried into the forests by ancestors of the Akan, Yoruba, Edo and others, who claim a northerly, possibly Nilotic, origin for their culture.[18] We do know that more than seven thousand years ago, Egyptian houses were rectangular with open courtyards. Kushitic palaces at Meroë followed a similar pattern. Then again, it is also tempting to point to possible origins in Roman North Africa where impluvial forms flourished along the Mediterranean littoral.[19]

The impluvium form reached its highest point of articulation in the cities of the Yoruba and Asante in the early nineteenth century. Yet even by that time new European styles had begun to penetrate the forest cities. They followed along the lines of coastal stone fortresses and warehouses. European styles were at first not very common. An observer in 1562 described the houses at Elmina as "made all of canes and reeds."[20] As late as 1702 Bosman noted that most African houses along the Gold Coast were "round at the top and encompassed by mud walls. . . ."[21] However, by the mid-nineteenth century Fante masons were already at work in the Asante capital at Kumasi, introducing European coastal styles.[22]

Two story timber buildings were not common in the forested areas of West Africa until the nineteenth century. This may partly be attributed to the rather recent introduction of brick-making, which did not appear in Yorubaland until about 1850. Formerly, buildings were of reinforced bulk-earth construction. After midcentury, it became fashionable for Obas (chiefs) to live in such structures because

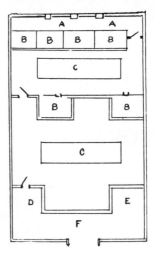

58. Sketch plan of a typical Benin city house by C. Punch in 1891. H. Ling Roth, *Great Benin*, Barnes and Noble reprint, 1968.

A cooking areas
B storage rooms
C inner impluvial courtyards
D porch
E religious altar
F entrance court

they satisfied the social need for greater elevation. Two-story house styles were probably first introduced by Yoruba-descended liberated slaves returning from South America and Sierra Leone. The so-called "Brazilian" houses became popular in Lagos after 1900, and the style spread inland with cocoa prosperity.[23]

Rectangular buildings did not become common in small towns and villages in most of sub-Saharan Africa until the colonial era, when large numbers of them were constructed by missionaries, Arab/Swahili traders, and colonial officials. Suddenly rectilinear forms became a symbol of wealth, worldliness, urbanity, and political power. No longer did people desire a circular hut within a round compound. Progress and prestige were rectangular and, if possible, two story. A corrugated metal roof became a necessity; such a roof made rectangular construction easier, faster, and more permanent. Today, in the northern forests of West Africa, round houses are fast disappearing. Coastward, circular structures are now limited to an occasional religious hut or a fish-smoking oven. Only in the savanna do they persist; and there they are found mostly among non-Muslim peasant groups.

In some societies, the cylinder coexists with the square or the rectangle. In Nyakyusa villages of Tanzania, the senior wives still dwell in round houses.[24] Likewise in Dagomba villages of northern Ghana women live in round houses, while the young men prefer their own rectangular room-units. Labelle Prussin explains that the rectangular forms "are probably the result of contact with southern Gha-

59. Yoruba town-house, reminiscent of Afro-Brazilian architecture (Ibadan city, Nigeria). Author's photo.

60. Dagomba compound (northern Ghana). Author's photo.

naian building, which many of the young men . . . have seen during their annual dry-season migration to the cities on the coast."[25] Despite European influence—and in South Africa it has been present for more than 300 years—many Africans choose to remain in their circular mud-and-thatch structures. They are at once utilitarian, comfortable, and esthetically pleasing. However, there is little doubt that the long-term trend is toward rectangular forms.

① DOMICAL (beehive)

② CONE ON CYLINDER

③ CONE ON POLES AND MUD CYLINDER

④ GABLE ROOFED (rectangular)

⑤ PYRAMIDAL CONE

⑥ RECTANGLE WITH ROOF ROUNDED AND SLOPING AT THE ENDS

⑦ SQUARE

⑧ DOME OR FLAT ROOF ON A CLAY BOX (quadrangular or square)

⑨ QUADRANGULAR, SURROUNDING AN OPEN COURTYARD

⑩ CONE ON GROUND

MAJOR STRUCTURAL FORMS OF PRECOLONIAL AFRICAN DWELLINGS.

[1] James Walton, African Village (Pretoria, 1956), pp. 127–28.

[2] Ioan Thomas, "The Flat-Roofed Houses of the Sebei at Benet," Uganda Journal 27, no. 1 (1963), 109–14. Before the advent of Christianity in Axum, all public buildings had a square as their basis. See David Buxton, The Abyssinians (New York, 1970), p. 92.

[3] Oliver Davies, West Africa Before the Europeans (London, 1967), p. 227. See also P. C. Ozanna, "Ghana," in P. L. Shinnie, ed., The African Iron Age (Oxford, 1971), p. 44; J. D. Clark, "Mobility and Settlement Patterns in sub-Saharan Africa," in: Peter J. Ucko, ed., Man, Settlement and Urbanism (London, 1972), p. 134.

[4] I. Kimambo, "The Pare," in A. Roberts, ed., Tanzania before 1900 (Nairobi, 1968), pp. 31–32.

[5] A. Roberts, "The Nyamwezi," Ibid., pp. 117–33; F. W. H. Migeod, Across Equatorial Africa (London, 1923), p. 294.

[6] Ibid., p. 294.

[7] Joseph Thomson, To the Central African Lakes and Back (London, 1881), 2: 88–91.

[8] The Church Missionary Gleaner, October, 1893, p. 156.

[9] Harry Johnston, George Grenfell and the Congo (1908; reprinted New York, 1969), 2:749.

[10] Ibid., 2:753.

[11] Ibid., 2:739.

[12] J. R. Willis, "The Spread of Islam" in Adu Boahen et al., ed., Horizon History of Africa (New York, 1971), p. 147.

[13] David Etherton, "Algerian Oases," in Paul Oliver, ed., Shelter in Africa (New York, 1971), p. 183.

[14] Personal field notes, Kano, 6 August 1966.

[15] Nehemiah Levtzion, Ancient Ghana and Mali (London, 1973), p. 231.

[16] Oral Testimony, Mallam Urwatu, 4 July 1966.

[17] E. W. Bovill, ed., Missions to the Niger (London, 1966), 4:698.

[18] Labelle Prussin, Architecture in Northern Ghana (Los Angeles, 1969), p. 92, attributes the wide dispersal of mosques to the Islamic Mande Dyula. Phyllis Ferguson ("Mosques and Islamization Process in the 19th Century among the Eastern Dyula" [unpubl. ms.]) traces the Maghribi-Andalusian mosque forms to the western Sudan in the fourteenth century. From Mali they apparently spread to Kong and were ultimately carried southward by the Mande Dyula traders.

[19] D. P. Addy, "The Study of Thermal Comfort in Traditional Houses in Ghana" (M.S. thesis, Kumasi, 1969), p. 40.

[20] J. W. Blake, European Beginnings in West Africa (London, 1937), p. 360.

[21] Willem Bosman, A New and Accurate Description of the Coast of Guinea (London, 1705; reprinted 1968), p. 477.

[22] Winwood Reade, The Story of the Ashantee Campaign (London, 1874), p. 357.

[23] Eva Krapf-Askari, *Yoruba Towns and Cities* (Oxford, 1969), p. 59. Two-story houses were introduced into Uganda by Protestant missionaries when in 1895 they built a house for Kabaka Mwanga of Buganda. See *Church Missionary Gleaner*, May 1895, p. 69. Also note in this passage that bulk earth construction predominated in Asante until the colonial era, when sun-dried bricks became popular. (See Adu Ameyaw, "Ashanti Traditional Religious Architecture" [M.S. thesis, Kumasi, 1967]).

[24] Personal field notes, Dar es Salaam, 11 August 1970.

[25] See Prussin, *Architecture in Northern Ghana*.

4

TOWN AND SOCIETY

Social and Political Structures

HUMAN and structural contours of African towns and cities were dictated by a wide variety of factors, including geography, kinship organization, and political and occupational orientation. The basic unit of African society, the extended family, was reflected in the overall pattern of urban living. Private dwellings were often situated according to relationships created by clannic affiliations. And the very design of buildings mirrored not only family and tribal structure but religious, political, and economic institutions. As Labelle Prussin states, "Architecture, and by extension environmental design in spatial terms, is the making visible of the 'ethnic domain'. The way space and people in space are organized reflects values, life styles, status. It is a physical reflection of social networks."[1] African urban agglomerations are indeed the physical projection into space of the social, economic, and political organization of its inhabitants. Urban elites, in situating community structures, usually paid greater attention to human relationships than to geometric design.

African towns and cities contained diverse clusters of households,

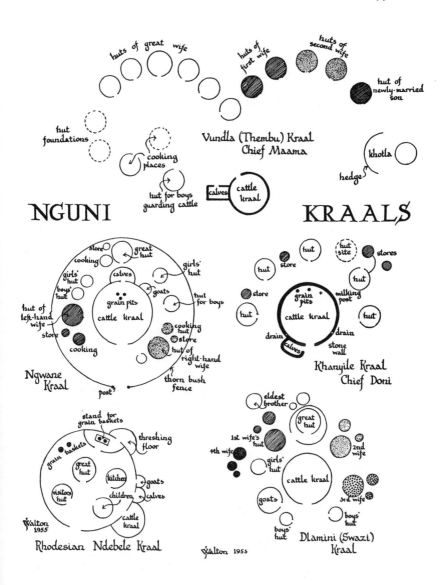

61. Nguni kraals (South Africa). J. L. Van Schaik, *African Village*, James Walton, Cape Town, 1956.

each cluster composing a ward. Authority within a given ward ema-
nated from a council of household elders under the leadership of a
head elder or chief. Depending on the city or state, ward identity
might be based on one or more considerations: ethnic, military,
occupational, social, or religious. Wards were further combined into
political quarters in the larger African communities.

In large towns, a plethora of wards may exist with each ward
possessing a distinct ethnic identity. Precolonial Kano held 127 wards,
one of the earliest being occupied by the Hausa.[2] After about 1450,
new wards were created for the Fulani immigrants. During the period
from the institutionalization of Islam (ca. 1500) until the time of the
Fulani Holy War (1804), ethnic groups other than the Hausa settled
within Kano city: Yoruba in Ayagi ward, Nupe in Tudun Nufawa
ward, and Ghadames and Tripolitan Arabs in Dandalin Turawa
ward.[3] After the Fulani *jihad*, these groups were followed by communities of Tuareg, Kanuri, and others. Hausa cities tended to be

62. Precolonial city layouts, showing quarters reserved for different ethnic
groups and the situation of mosques and markets. L. G. Binger, *Voyage du
Niger au Golfe de Guinée*, Paris, 1888.

a. Kong—(northern Ivory Coast) A large caravan city which reached its
zenith in the eighteenth century.

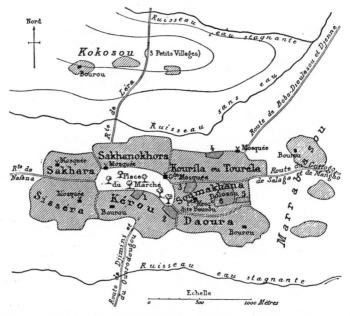

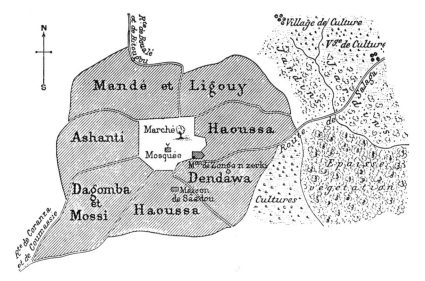

b. Kintampo—Market town north of the Asante Union. It prospered in the late nineteenth century.

c. Bondoukou—Caravan city which also lay to the north of Asante. It traded with the Gold Coast towns as well as Djenné northwards on the Niger River. Along with King, it traded in kola nuts, gold, and slaves.

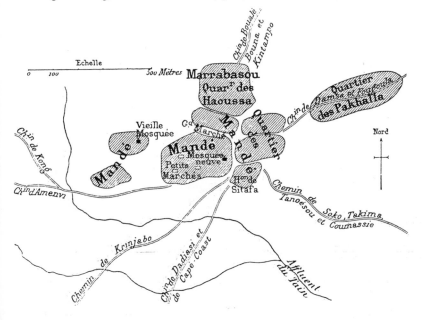

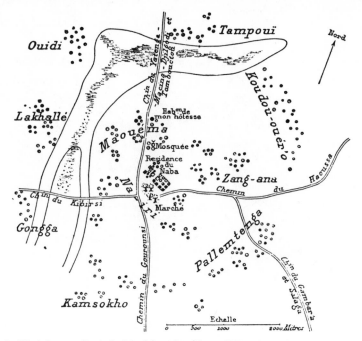

d. Wagadugu—Capital of the Mossi kingdom of Wagadugu, founded probably in the mid-fifteenth century (Upper Volta).

multi-ethnic with centralized municipal control in the hands of a Magajin Gari, or "Mayor of the Town." He in turn was responsible to the Emir (king) of the entire state, who resided in an extensive walled palace compound near the city's center. After the *jihad* (around 1804–10) all positions of power fell to the Fulani victors. The Emir and his Council of State were thenceforth members of the Fulani ethnic group. But now the Emir of each kingdom (Emirate) was ultimately responsible to the Caliph of the entire Sokoto Caliphate, who resided in Sokoto city.

Benin city, on the other hand, was overwhelmingly of a single ethnic group, the Edo. For centuries, the city was organized into wards based exclusively upon crafts (which began with skills such as wood- and ivory-carving) and ritual priesthoods connected with ancestor worship. At the center of urban authority was the Oba, or king, who also ruled over the entire realm. This divine monarch was surrounded by nonhereditary palace chiefs and town chiefs and hereditary titled nobles.[4] The latter were a kind of third force between the palace and the town chiefs. The authority of the nobles extended beyond the capital to the outlying towns and villages where they resided. By the seventeenth century, the town chiefs as individuals also shared in the government of surrounding towns and villages. Indeed, the Oba's main political weapon lay in his ability to manipulate the system of Palace and Town offices. [5] Moreover, much of Benin's political history turns upon the efforts of important men and families to win a place or to advance in the hierarchies of town and palace, and upon the attempts of rulers and pretenders to the throne to consolidate a following in those associations. [6]

Little information exists on the social and political structure of Old Oyo before its total destruction in the early nineteenth century. However, it is believed that New Oyo's institutions were patterned along the lines of its predecessor. After about 1860, New Oyo was subdivided into wards, the royal wards headed by titled nobles and the others by members of the Council of State, or Oyo Mesi. The Oyo Mesi's seven titled positions were held by powerful land-owning lineages. At the center of the city was the divine king, or Alafin, who also held sway over the provincial towns and villages. Between the Alafin and the Oyo Mesi stood the Ogboni Cult of the Earth, which acted as a check on the other two branches. As worshippers of the earth spirits, the Ogboni enjoyed both religious and political power. [7]

Oyo city was linked to towns and villages throughout the empire by transforming local chiefs into clients of the Alafin and other notables residing in the capital. According to Robert Smith, "The system of government of the capital was repeated on a smaller scale in the provincial towns of the kingdom, and paralleled also in the subject kingdoms."[8] Towns themselves were graded into a hierarchy of political categories. Major towns—*i.e.*, administrative headquarters, were defined as "crowned towns" (*ilu alade*). Communities under their jurisdiction were called "towns on the fringe of farmland" (*ilu ereko*). *Obas* (mayors) of these towns were not permitted to wear a beaded crown. Within the category of *ilu ereko* fell the market-towns, villages, hamlets and encampments. [9] Rev. Samuel Johnson, the great nineteenth-century scholar of Yoruba civilization, noted that the village must necessarily be subordinate to the nearest town from which it sprang, and in this way an embryo town is formed. However, he cautioned, "There are cases in which an influential personage with a large following deliberately built a town, and is from the beginning recognised head of the same. . . ."[10]

The division within Yoruba towns and cities was mainly by social stratification. At Ife, nine social strata could be identified. New Oyo had four major social categories: aristocrats, free commoners, eunuchs, and slaves.

With the advent of civil war in the nineteenth century, the situation changed. At Ibadan, for example, urban dwellers looked not to kinship but to the army groups as their social units.[11] At Kumasi, capital of the Asante confederacy, city wards were under the control of titled warlords (Nsafohene) who answered directly to the king, or Asantehene. These ward heads exercised considerable influence over both the capital and the confederacy as a whole. In the early nineteenth century they constituted a political cadre capable of a considerable degree of independent action.[12] The city itself contained seventy-seven wards; preeminent among them was Bantama, whose chief was senior commander of the armed forces. His rank around 1817 was second only to that of the Asantehene. Throughout the nineteenth century the Kumasi Nsafohene and the chiefs of the outlying provinces (Amanhene) competed for power and privilege.

Administratively speaking, the capital city and outlying towns and villages in Africa were often linked by requirements that fiefholders reside for a certain period each year at the capital and within proximity of the royal compound. These hereditary landed aristocrats initially served as a major channel of communication between the city authorities and the subject masses in the countryside. Yet, inevitably, kings would also appoint their own retainers, usually slaves, to oversee local affairs, particularly in the newly conquered areas. Many titled aristocrats, inured to the pleasures of urban life and the beneficence of the monarch, were thus able to become absentee landlords, preferring to spend most of their time at the capital. This trend seemed most evident in the Emirates of the Sokoto Caliphate from the mid-nineteenth century. However, the phenomenon was fairly common to other centralized polities south of the Sahara.

Patterns of Segregation

Patterns of segregation clearly existed in many African towns and cities. They were manifested most glaringly in the phenomenon of bifurcated communities. Al-Bakri, the eleventh-century Arab geographer from Cordoba, described Ghana's capital of Kumbi-Saleh in 1067–68 as essentially two towns, one Muslim and immigrant, the other indigenous with a traditional religious outlook.

The city of Ghana consists of two towns in a plain. One of these towns is inhabited by Muslims. It is large with a dozen mosques in one which they assemble for the Friday prayer. . . . The royal town . . . . is six miles away [from the Muslim town], and the area between the two towns is covered with houses. Their houses are made of stone and acacia wood. The king has a palace and conical huts, surrounded by a wall-like enclosure. In the king's town, not far from the royal court of justice, is a mosque where pray the Muslims who come there on missions. [13]

When the Portuguese reached what would become Elmina on the Gold Coast in about 1482 they discovered a large village in two parts with a different cultural group in each. [14] Indeed, the phenomenon of bifurcated communities was found throughout sub-Saharan Africa where different groups came together to live and work. Great Zimbabwe was essentially in two parts, the royal acropolis on the hill, and the Great Enclosure in the valley where the masses resided and conducted market activity. In this case it was a division between the sacred and the profane, the spiritual and the commercial. A later example of twin-city development may be found at Kukawa, capital of nineteenth-century Bornu in West Africa. Kukawa was rebuilt in the 1850s and laid out as a twin city. The eastern half was reserved for wealthy residents (kings, leading chiefs, and merchants), while the western half, separated by a cleared open space approximately a half-mile long, was crowded and poor, with narrow, winding alleys. The two parts of the city were connected by a wide road, lined with occasional strings of detached dwellings. [15]

Nonfree groups in many African polities were forced to live in separate residential areas. Until quite recently, most Kalahari villages in southern Africa contained pockets of unassimilated foreign communities in addition to the locally dominant ethnic group. Bushmen, for example, had to live as serfs on the periphery of the Bantu communities. They would enter their master's village to fulfill seasonal demands for labor but were denied a voice in village politics, being regarded by the Bantu villagers as ugly and inferior. [16]

A similar condition prevailed in seventh-century Old Calabar in the Niger Delta of West Africa. Efik society was based on kinship, which determined a resident's membership in family, compound, and lineage. The slaves were considered outsiders and enjoyed no economic, social, or political rights. [17] Yet, like the Bushmen, they were expected to identify with the interests of their masters. Nearby in Iboland, the houses of the slaves (Osu) were always situated away from the master's compound. Any free person who married an Osu was socially ostracized; and it was to prevent such occurrences that the Osu were physically segregated from their master's residence. Free Ibo men practiced a remarkably sophisticated form of democracy, though they denied equal opportunity to their slaves.

Residential segregation did not apply exclusively to fellow Africans. Light-skinned Egyptians and North Africans, referred to as whites, had to reside in a separate quarter at the capital of Mali in the fourteenth century. In the Niger River city of Gao, whites possessed their own mosque and in legal matters had to refer to specially appointed judges.[18] In sixteenth-century Mbanza Kongo, European newcomers were geographically separated from other townsmen by royal order.[19] Obviously Europeans, when in power, tended to develop their own segregationist policies. The Dutch East India settlement at Table Bay in South Africa was racially segregated almost from its conception. Governor Jan vanRiebeeck in 1657 planted a hedge enclosing six thousand acres, the original nucleus of Cape Town, and reserved it exclusively for whites.[20] But physical and legal barriers anywhere in Africa seldom completely prevent different racial or ethnic groups from interacting. Widespread interbreeding occurred not only between so-called whites and blacks in the cities of the West African Sudan; it also prevailed for nearly two centuries in the Cape Town vicinity, where Europeans, Malays, Khoikhoi (Hottentots) and San (Bushmen) melted into a new ethnic group called the "Cape Colored."

Segregation did not confine itself to race, ethnicity, or culture; nor was it always involuntary. In the Nyakyusa region of southern Tanzania, young men voluntarily moved away from their parents' homes to establish their own separate, age-set villages. Lucy Mair wrote, "An age-set village recruits members for five to seven years; after that the next batch of boys ready to leave home must start a new one. So at any time there are a number of villages with a recognised order of seniority."[21] In the larger Nyakyusa communities or towns, life was oriented along a broad road with dwellings grouped on each side according to age. Nearby Sukuma towns were divided into sections, called *vibanda*, with each section retaining a specific age group.

Nyakyusa and Sukuma social organization may have served to reduce generational conflicts. It was also a convenient and efficient means of mobilizing labor for communal work. [22]

Within larger African towns, ghettoes developed as a natural outgrowth of human migrations and patterns of trade. A newcomer to an urban center usually chose to reside among people sharing a single language, culture, or occupation. Ghettoes rarely seemed oppressive, because the mechanisms of social control lay in the hands of their residents. Moreover, families usually owned their own buildings, provided for much of their own security, and operated within an institutional framework created by their ancestors.

Community control was taken for granted because leaders sprang from within resident families. Consequently, intergroup and interpersonal conflicts could be resolved by clan elders or other local officials. Power therefore rested with the people, and only problems transcending the ward or quarter devolved upon the king or the hereditary municipal leader and his councillors. Warlords were the municipal leaders among the indigenous Yoruba in Ibadan; foreign elements in the city had their own intermediaries. For example, the Hausa lived in a special quarter headed not by a Yoruba but by a Hausa chief who enjoyed the sanction of the local Yoruba municipal authorities. [23]

African leaders, as trustees of the first ancestral settlers, could create new quarters or, if necessary, new towns for new immigrants, because allocation of living space usually rested in their hands. The ancestors were the real, legal landowners. Rattray, in describing the traditional Asante conception of land, stated:

> The Ashanti [sic] land laws . . . [are] the logical outcome of a belief which . . . considered the living landowners as but holding as it were tenancies at will from the dead, and as being trustees of the latter. . . . it may be this religious aspect which largely accounts for the reluctance in the West African mind to the total alienation by sale of land to a foreigner. . . . [24]

To the Asante, as to many African societies, the soil was regarded as a deity, a goddess who could be neither bought nor sold. Thus, when a stranger "purchased" or was allocated land, he came into possession only of the *use* of the land. African strangers to traditional towns and cities understood this principle clearly. But, as K. Y. Daaku noted, this concept of African land tenure created problems later in relations between Europeans and Africans. The Europeans operated under the assumption that the chiefs owned the land. Not infrequently, chiefs granted concessions to Europeans in return for gifts. These concessions were not intended, however, to transfer to Europeans any fundamental rights to the land.[25]

The ceremonial, spiritual cities, whether dispersed or compact, showed little tendency to absorb excess rural population. Nor did they display an inclination to permit large numbers of foreigners to settle within their urban limits. Authorities in Kumasi, Abomey, Benin, Ife, Great Zimbabwe, and elsewhere placed severe restrictions on foreign settlement and activities. Thus, through land-allocation powers, urban leaders were able to exert a degree of population control and central planning.

We have already noted that chiefs regulated the movement of traffic into their walled market towns by constructing gates and toll houses. Visitors were identified and their baggage inspected. Normally, duties were levied on each marketable item. Before the age of imperialism, European traders and explorers humbly sought royal assent before entering a major town, and while visiting, they were politely constrained to reside in royally designated compounds.

The Town and the Countryside

Traditional African towns and cities contained many internally self-governing communities within a single administrative and geographical entity. Yet the cohesion of lineal, ethnic, and religious groups within each quarter or ward discouraged social deviance and promoted strong feelings of corporate responsibility. Furthermore, traditional urbanization did not weaken kinship bonds or fragment small lineage structures. Lineages remained united in extensive compounds, and these compounds shared common values and beliefs. Towns and cities were thus structured so as to provide dwellers with a deep sense of personal identity and security.

In large territorial polities, the seat of government was divided into sections corresponding to provincial governing units. This system enabled paramount chiefs in outlying provinces to exert authority over a quarter within the central capital. Such a quarter contained the chief s own subjects, living temporarily or permanently at the capital.

In this sense, a town or city was both a macrocosm of the small family compound and a microcosm of the kingdom itself. Many urban elites never completely lost sight of this duality. Some rulers, upon their installation, traveled to the southern, northern, eastern, and western corners of the capital in order to demonstrate symbolically their possession of the entire kingdom.

While African towns and cities may have achieved some degree of internal integration, their relationship with smaller rural communities was not always harmonious. Religious and ethnic homogeneity in many parts of Yorubaland may have indeed contributed to the urban dweller's view of the countryside as an extension of the town; Yoruba urbanites were linked to rural people by socioreligious ties.[26] However, in areas of great religious, ethnic, and linguistic diversity, and where there were people of different cultural heritages, profound differences existed between urban dwellers and rural folk. These contrasts were most apparent in Islamized urban centers. Muslim residents of East African coastal cities and their savanna counterparts in West Africa looked down upon their less cosmopolitan relatives who clung to customary legal and religious procedures and operated within indigenous institutions of government. In Songhay, the Askia Muhammad Touré found this difference to be a serious impediment to nation integration. Muhammad Touré was a devout Muslim of foreign birth from a distant tributary state. However, his palace coup in 1493 enjoyed the enthusiastic support of Islamic merchants and scholars in the major urban areas such as Timbuktu, Djenné, and Gao. Yet, clearly, Muhammad Touré had no legitimate claim to the throne, and he was considered a usurper by Songhay's non-Muslim majorities. He therefore turned to Islam to reinforce his authority. He devoted his greatest energies in the urban areas, in the mosques and the marketplaces, where he knew his strength lay. In other words, he sought to establish an effective power base among the market people and the urban masses, many of whom were linked by family and commerce to Muslim North Africa. Freed from the traditions of the past, Touré, whose reign continued to 1528, could innovate and introduce Islamic institutions. Songhay's cities began to acquire a unity of architecture, religion, education, law, and government—all based on Islamic principles. The cities of the Songhay empire became cosmopolitan centers where merchants and scholars from distant lands congregated and exchanged ideas and commodities. Rural folk, on the other hand, remained little touched; and they resented the growing power and influence of the Muslim-dominated urban centers. Unwittingly, the Askia had created a destructive conflict between the traditional ruralist and the Islamic urbanite, a conflict that in the years between 1528 and the Moroccan invasion of 1591 would eat away the fabric of the empire.[27]

African urban life in general tended to accentuate differences in sociopolitical status. One's standing in the community was often reflected in house style, building materials, and in some cases the dwelling's proximity to the royal compound. Most palaces in seventeenth-century Benin city were decorated with a small pyramidal turret·topped by a cast snake or a bird with outspread wings. The exterior walls were of deep red clay, ribbed or fluted horizontally so as to resemble brickwork. The richness of the wall coloring was achieved by mixing the clay with animal blood. Of course, only the very wealthy could afford such a luxury.[28] According to Frank Willett, "The Palace of the king of Benin was built with thicker walls than other buildings, with a greater number of courses (seven or more) of mud, and thus a greater height than those of other people's houses."[29] In Abomey, capital of the kingdom of Dahomey, no one could construct a house of more than four tiers of mud swish, and in Kumasi, Benin, and Abomey, two-story houses were the exclusive right of the monarchs. Archibald Dalzel observed in about 1790 that at Abomey the king possessed a "large building, of two stories, and about thirty or forty feet high; so that the top of it may be seen from without. This house seems to be intended more for show than use; for the king never dwells in it."[30] The *afins*, or palace compounds, of the Obas of Yoruba towns had a distinctive *kobi*, which resembled a porch. This extension of the verandah allowed rulers greater space in their courtyards for public receptions. *Kobis* were highly regarded as architectural marks of rank, and only the houses of Obas and a few other high ranking officials could possess them.[31]

In many African communities, dwellings were arranged spatially on the basis of the occupant's political or social status. In Yoruba towns, the Oba's *afin* was situated in the center of the town, next to the marketplace. Surrounding the *afin* were the compounds of those serving the Oba. The varying distances of the compounds from the *afin* revealed the occupant's position in the government hierarchy. In

63. Asante dwellings (central Ghana). Note the courses, or tiers, of mud walling. Author's photo.

64. Intricately carved door, common to many town-houses in Zanzibar and in major East African coastal towns. Author's photo.

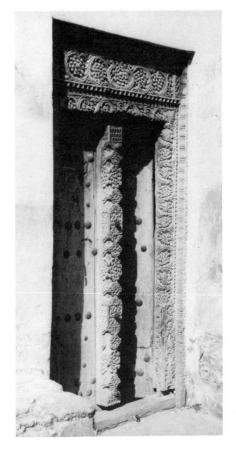

65. The Asantehene's
(king's) guest house in
about 1874. Designs in
mud walls were exe-
cuted in high relief.
Richard Austin Free-
man, *Travels and Life
in Ashanti and Jaman*,
London, 1898.

66. Frieze of a royal Asante guest house (late nineteenth century). Freeman,
Travels and Life.

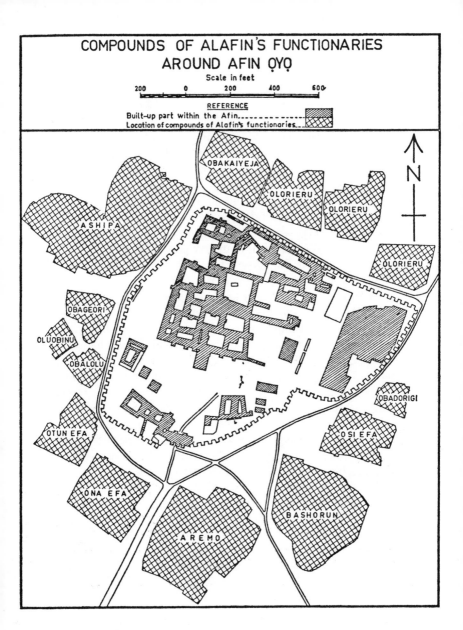

COMPOUNDS OF ALAFIN'S FUNCTIONARIES AROUND AFIN ỌYỌ

Scale in feet

200   0   200   400   600

REFERENCE

Built-up part within the Afin..........

Location of compounds of Alafin's functionaries....

OBAKAIYEJA

OLORIERU

OLORIERU

OLORIERU

ASHIPA

N

OBAGEORI

OLUOBINU

OBALOLU

OBADORIGI

OTUN EFA

OSI EFA

ONA EFA

BASHORUN

AREMO

67. Compounds of Alafin's functionaries around Afin (palace), Oyo. Courtesy University of London Press, G. J. A. Ojo, *Yoruba Palaces*, London, 1966.

southern Africa, Zulu kraals were organized in two distinct branches. Houses on the right branch (*eku Nene*) extended in a line from the kraal entrance up to and including the Great Hut or *iNdlunkulu*, which stood at the top of the circular settlement. The *eku Nene* huts were occupied by the major wives, with the great wife in charge of the *iNdlunkulu*. The left side of the walled circular enclosure contained the habitations of the lesser wives. The entire layout articulated a design intended to minimize social friction and to assign every family member his or her rightful place. Moreover, it ensured an orderly succession upon the death of the kraal leader. The kraal's layout was a physical expression of the institution of polygamy. It exemplified the mother's ambitions for her son's future as well as the son's desires to succeed to his father's position of leadership.[32]

In African towns and cities the geometry of the layout determined the nature of opportunities for social and economic intercourse. For privacy, African compounds usually looked inward upon an open courtyard. This inner space provided a communal area for washing, cooking, craftwork, relaxation, and perhaps prayer. The typical compound in West Africa's savanna was entered through an entrance building called a *zaure* by the Hausa. These large, high-ceilinged structures served the compound head as a workshop for weaving, a learning center for boys, or a meeting-place and dining room for his male guests. The *zaure* led into a forecourt (*kofar gida*), from which one had to pass through a second entrance hall before reaching the heart of the compound. At the center were the dwellings of the compound head and his wives, children, and immediate relatives. There were also separate units for storage (granaries, etc.) and cooking. The most common organization of a compound was that each wife had a cluster of units reserved for her own use. The compound head possessed his own sleeping unit and another for his guests. Together, they were located in his own small courtyard. The entire compound was completely enclosed by a continuous wall, which also served to connect the interior dwellings. Screened-off subdivisions provided privacy for bathing.

It should be recalled that clusters of compounds were usually grouped into wards. Every ward had its own community wells, marketplace, and center of worship. Groups of wards, or quarters, were separated from each other by broad avenues or corridors, which

68. Painting designs on a wall of Ndebele dwelling (South Africa). Author's photo.

69. The Asantehene's sleeping room within his palace compound in Kumasi (early nineteenth century). T. Edward Bowdich, *Mission from Cape Coast Castle to Ashantee*, London, 1819.

converged at a large open community space in the heart of the town or city. Surrounding that public space were the chiefs or king's compound, a central marketplace, and, if the town was a seat of territorial government, the homes of leading aristocratic families and dignitaries. Thus, the urban dweller could be as public or private as he or she wished. But divine kingship, where it thrived, often led to the creation of cities within cities in order to preserve the secrecy of power. The divine king's compound became in effect a private city, open only to his personal retainers (usually slaves), leading chiefs, and invited visitors. This was indeed privacy at its ultimate.

In conclusion, it would appear that the cohesion of lineages in urban areas obviated instability, insecurity, criminality, and violence. True, ghettoes did exist in large towns and cities, monarchs sometimes monopolized homesite allocations and separated themselves from the exploited masses, and patterns of segregation—social, racial, ethnic, and religious—were not uncommon. Yet urban dwelling did not become oppressive, nor did it weaken kinship bonds or lineage structures. Indeed, urban social cohesion prevailed in black Africa until the twentieth-century colonial era. To use a Mumfordian evaluation, "the city did not become a city-region: open-ended, bereft of its walls, whether real or imagined."[33] Nor were precolonial cities and towns amorphous, without a sense of identity or purpose. Urban precolonial Africa was an exciting, civilized, cosmopolitan arena which fired the imagination and enthusiasm of most foreign visitors.

A certain reassuring quality of familial intimacy prevailed in precolonial African towns and cities. Most urbanites were born, raised, married, reared children, grew old, and died within the confines of a given quarter or ward. If anything, family and lineage connections were strengthened by urban living. Towns and cities were not the abode of a faceless, anomic human mass. Rather, they comprised a dynamic mélange of cohesive families and lineages. In their own quarters or wards, urban dwellers knew and respected each other's person and property. Each quarter or ward generated a strong sense of corporate identity and community responsibility; and in turn each one respected the integrity of neighboring wards. But when faced with problems involving the welfare of the entire community, everyone worked together. In nineteenth-century Yorubaland, when a town had expanded to the limits of its walls, the town council would determine the amount of new area to be taken in. The entire town then participated in constructing a new wall. Everyone was involved, including women and children, who were responsible for hauling water which would be used in making a mud swish mixture for the new wall's surface.[34]

70. A group of women constructing a mud-cylinder for a new community dwelling (Venda, South Africa). Author's photo.

Thus, each corporate body identified with the city as a totality. This identification was undoubtedly made possible because everyone's voice was heard, through a chain of representation extending from the family head to the lineage head to the ward leader to the urban chiefs to the king's council and to the king. Nevertheless, not everyone enjoyed an equal voice. There were always limitations on privilege, based on such factors as age, sex, wealth, and the number of generations of one's lineage that had resided within the city walls.

[1] Labelle Prussin, "An Introduction to Indigenous African Architecture," *Journal of the Society of Architectural Historians* 33, no. 3 (1974), 192.

[2] John Paden, "Situational Ethnicity in Urban Africa with Special Reference to the Hausa" (unpublished ms., p. 13).

[3] *Ibid.*, p. 14.

[4] Alan Ryder, *Benin and the Europeans* (New York, 1969), p. 4. R. E. Bradbury, "Benin," in Darryl Forde and P. M. Kaberry, eds., *West African Kingdoms in the Nineteenth Century* (London, 1967), p. 12.

[5] *Ibid.*, p. 28.

[6] Ryder, *Benin and the Europeans*, p. 9.

[7] Peter Morton-Williams, "The Yoruba Kingdom of Oyo," in Forde and Kaberry, eds., *West African Kingdoms*, p. 50.

[8] Robert S. Smith, *Kingdoms of the Yoruba* (London, 1965), p. 45.

[9] *Ibid.*, p. 109.

[10] Samuel Johnson, *History of the Yorubas* (London, 1921), p. 90.

[11] W. C. Morgan and J. C. Pugh, *West Africa* (London, 1969), p. 52.

[12] Ivor Wilks, "Ashanti Government," in Forde and Kaberry, eds., *West African Kingdoms*, p. 226; William Tordoff, *Ashanti under the Prempehs* (London, 1965), p. 3.

[13] Nehemiah Levtzion, *Ancient Ghana and Mali* (London, 1973), p. 23.

[14] J. W. Blake, ed., *Europeans in West Africa* (London, 1942), p. 72.

[15] R. O. Collins, ed., *African History: Text and Readings* (New York, 1971), pp. 85–86.

[16] Adam Kuper, *Kalahari Village Politics* (London, 1970), p. 47.

[17] A. J. H. Latham, *Old Calabar 1600–1891* (Oxford, 1973), p. 32.

[18] Levtzion, *Ancient Ghana and Mali*, p. 197.

[19] Leo Africanus, *The History and Description of Africa* (London, 1896), 1, *Hakluyt*, 73.

[20] M. F. Katzen, "White Settlers and the Origin of a New Society," in: Monica Wilson and L. M. Thompson, eds., *Oxford History of South Africa* (Oxford, 1969), 1, 190.

[21] Lucy Mair, *African Societies* (London, 1974), p. 232.

[22] *Ibid.*

[23] Personal field notes, Kano, 6 June 1966.

[24] R. S. Rattray, *Ashanti* (1923; reprinted New York, 1969).

[25] K. Y. Daaku, *Trade and Politics on the Gold Coast 1600–1720* (London, 1970), p. 51.

[26] Eva Krapf-Askari, *Yoruba Towns and Cities* (Oxford, 1969), p. 44.

[27] J. O. Hunwick, "Religion and State in the Songhay Empire," in I. M. Lewis and D. Forde, eds., *Islam in Tropical Africa* (London, 1966), pp. 296–318.

[28] H. Ling Roth, *Great Benin* (1903; reprinted New York 1968), p. 181.

[29] Frank Willett, *African Art* (New York, 1971), p. 132.

[30] Archibald Dalzel, *The History of Dahomey* (1793; reprinted London, 1967), p. 49.

[31] G. J. A. Ojo, *Yoruba Palaces* (London, 1966), p. 58.

[32] Barrie Biermann, "Indlu: The Domed Dwelling of the Zulu," in Paul Oliver, ed., *Shelter in Africa* (New York, 1971), p. 100.

[33] Lewis Mumford, *The City in History* (New York, 1961), p. 517.

[34] Johnson, *History of the Yoruba*, p. 82.

5
THE LIFE AND DEATH
OF URBAN CENTERS

Economic Structure

URBAN rulers required wealth in order to survive. They needed a steady supply of revenue to support such essential services as the political bureaucracy; an army for security in markets and along trade routes; laborers to maintain roads, city walls, and public buildings; and a judiciary to settle disputes. These services were usually paid for by a system of taxation based on landholding, road tolls, external trade, and tribute in the form of agricultural goods, luxury items, coronation or installation fees, or slaves. Slaves were in great demand because in a preindustrial society manpower was the most important item of wealth a city could accumulate. Involuntary servitude was not uncommon to many precolonial African towns and cities, for without extensive monetary resources it was the easiest means of mobilizing labor to meet political and economic requirements. In most urban centers, servitude was accepted as a perfectly natural condition, and servants formed a high proportion of residential populations. They served in such capacities as municipal laborers, road and palace guards, eunuchs, and, in some societies, administrative watchdogs and tax collectors.

In the great commercial cities it was in the interests of urban rulers to closely supervise market activity and the movement of goods along the major trade arteries. Kings of Ghana and later Mali exerted a measure of control over the major market-towns and levied tolls on the road leading into and out of them. In medieval Ghana, the king demanded one dinar on every donkey-load of salt entering his lands and two dinars when it left. [1] Salt was in great demand by the perspiring gold miners of the southern forest, which lay beyond Ghana's political jurisdiction. To the miners, salt was worth its weight in gold. While gold dust itself passed tax-free through the western Sudanic markets, Ghanaian monarchs monopolized control of the less common nuggets; and in so doing they were able to regulate the country's monetary system. The city of Djenné may have developed as a commercial center for trade with the goldfields of the Akan forest. Traders carrying salt from the Taghaza mines in the Sahara met traders laden with forest gold. The wealth of Djenné and other western Sudanic cities rested in large measure on this vital exchange. [2] Yet the Sudanic cities could not have survived without produce from their agrarian hinterlands. And they did not hesitate to exploit the surrounding countryside in their search for financial and material support. Through taxation on agricultural produce, a portion of farm surpluses in Sudanic states was funneled into defraying the administrative costs of urban governments. To expand production, thereby creating necessary surpluses, Sudanic monarchs established new farming villages and placed their slaves in them. Surplus produce was stored in royal granaries and distributed by the urban leaders to their subordinates in return for loyalty and the performance of certain services.

Taxation dates far back into the history of the Hausa cities of northern Nigeria. Kano city began to impose a land tax in the thirteenth century and a cattle tax from about 1640 onwards. *Kurdin kasa*, a poll-tax or general tax on surrounding farming communities, was also introduced by Hausa urban elites at a very early date. [3]

In the larger African cities, occupational taxes were imposed on craftsmen and traders. Tax collection was entrusted to guild heads and others whose titles were bestowed on them by the king. In late-nineteenth-century Katsina city, a tax collector was assigned to each of the following occupations: blacksmiths; butchers; brokers and middlemen; manufacturers of farm tools; honey-makers; greengrocers; foreign merchants; cloth dyers; tanners; vendors of pumpkins, peanuts, cotton cloth, cassava, assorted nuts and salt. There was even a tax collector for "men who care for people bewitched by fairies." The revenue they collected went to support the urban administration and the king's huge personal staff, which embraced two secretaries; a court jester; a praise singer; a troupe of singers and dancers; several wind instrumentalists; numerous drummers; a counselor to the mentally ill; the palace police; a staff of housekeepers; a welfare officer in charge of the blind and indigent; a overseer of the lepers; an official who heard medical complaints; and keepers of the stables, public buildings, and city walls.[4]

Guilds in precolonial Africa were more common in towns and cities than in villages. Some of them extended across a number of communities, and tax-gatherers from the capital city were required to collect from them. Within an urban area, the various guilds, as previously mentioned, were localized into specific quarters, not uncommonly according to ethnic or kin groups. Thus, membership rested upon one's family background, not on talent alone.

Taxes on guilds, households, land, cattle, and agricultural produce did not suffice for the survival of all African metropolises. Dalzel, after a visit to Abomey, noted that the chief part of public revenue came from voluntary gifts paid by the subjects at an annual ceremony. Duties were also levied on captives taken in battles and raids by titled warlords. In addition, Dahomey had an annual capitation tax, an inheritance tax, a tax on palm-oil, tolls from trade routes, market dues, and import duties from specific items.[5] The wealth of city-states in the Niger Delta, before the era of palm-oil revenues, rested firmly on export earnings on slaves. John Adams, who carefully researched the city of Bonny between 1786 and 1800, found that no fewer than twenty thousand slaves were sold annually, sixteen thousand of whom were ethnic Ibos.[6]

The Niger Delta city-states were not the only ones to derive great municipal and private wealth from slave exports. It should be remembered that Old Oyo's prosperity rested on its position as the link between trade of the coast and that of the Sudanic cities to the north. The city exported slaves caught in the middle belt of Nigeria, and in its urban markets exchanged them for iron, salt, cutlasses, and imported cloth.

Rulers of many African cities, particularly administrative capitals, depended heavily on periodic tribute levied on conquered territories. Although this tribute often took the form of slaves, there were other items as well. Mbanza Kongo also received tribute in raphia cloth, ivory, and animal hides.[7] At Great Zimbabwe, the urban elites received cattle, copper, and gold. In Kumasi, tribute was demanded in gold whenever possible. Otherwise, the Asantehene settled for yards of fine cloth, livestock, or slaves.[8] In the late nineteenth century, Dahomey annually sent two hundred slaves to the municipal authorities in Kumasi as a form of friendly tribute.[9]

In the cities of Hausaland and, indeed, in many African cities, landed chiefs were obliged to supply their king with a portion of taxes collected from local peasants and to furnish him with a periodic supply of laborers. Corvee labor was often used to repair city walls and public buildings and to clear caravan routes. In Benin city, streets and markets were cleaned by teams of women, though this practice seems to be the exception.[10]

Not all urban administrative subordinates received regular compensation from the central treasury. In nineteenth-century Kumasi, they relied in large measure on fixed commissions and fees. A European observed that the king would give gold to his young, rising military subordinates in the form of a two- or three-year loan. Upon its expiration, the subordinate was expected not only to restore the principal but to demonstrate that he had accrued enough profit from it "to support the greater dignity the king would confer on him."[11]

Kings of Asante, Dahomey, and Benin established state monopolies over external trade which was geared to the needs of their capital city and the palace compound within. In Benin, long-distance trade was monopolized by various trading associations, many based in Benin city and all under the rigid control of the Oba. Trade itself was highly protectionist. Government agents were dispatched to the coast to inspect all arriving cargoes. After the value of each article had been assessed, duty had to be paid. The price, once established, could not be increased. After the Oba's agents had made their own commercial transactions, trade was thrown open to the general public. However, it was extremely difficult for foreign traders, particularly Europeans, to operate in Benin's interior markets. Gwato was the only port of European entry; nearly all other cities were off limits.[12] Foreigners wishing to visit Benin city needed the Oba's permission and had to agree not to engage in commercial activity.

A similar situation prevailed in the kingdom of Dahomey. The flourishing port city of Whydah came under Dahomean rule after the conquest of the Whydasians in 1727. Conquest was necessary because

Whydah's ruler had closed the port to Dahomean trade. Dahomey's capital, Abomey, lay landlocked some 150 miles from the coast. Despite the Dahomean takeover, Whydah's warehouses and markets continued to bustle with European traders from many nations. But Abomey, the cradle of Fon culture, remained inaccessible to Westerners. Dahomey's rulers feared the corrupting effects of Westernization and the cosmopolitan multicultural nature of Whydah. Control over the port city was seen as necessary only because of its outlet for exports and its source for imported military weapons, so vital to the kingdom's defenses. Whydah remained a free port to Europeans, though closed to almost all Dahomeans. Likewise, residents of Whydah were sealed off from the rest of the kingdom. The city of Whydah was governed as a "white man's town" through an African Viceroy directly responsible to the Dahomean king. Each of the clusters of European warehouses and residences constituted a separate ward and was usually administered by a Dahomey-appointed European. By the mid-nineteenth century, on the eve of the European conquest, there were four major "white man's" wards: Portuguese Town, Brazilian Town, English Town, and French Town. Europeans were left to their own commercial affairs in Whydah but were barred from trading in the interior. Internal trade was therefore entirely under Dahomean control.

Many Sudanic monarchs in the West African grasslands also opened their international urban market cities to foreigners. This was particularly true of the Songhay empire in the mid-sixteenth century. Similar to Whydah and Gwato in Dahomey and Benin, Kabara was the port city for an interior capital—in this case Timbuktu. Timbuktu was situated a number of miles off the Niger River, safe from periodic flooding. Even Kabara was a short distance from the river itself and was connected by a man-made canal. But these two Sudanic cities differed from their forest counterparts in that they were accessible to everyone relatively free from government control over their economic activity. In the Songhay empire, urban revenue was derived mainly from taxes and customs, not from direct government participation in the trade. Foreign merchants in Sudanic cities moved around the empire with greater ease than in Dahomey and Benin, and in the major towns and cities they became enormously influential in governing circles.

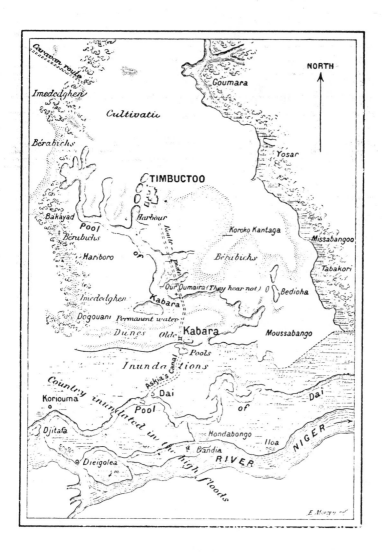

71. Timbuktu was located a short distance off the Niger River, safely above the flood plain. A twelve-mile canal was dug by the Askia Muhammad of Songhay in about 1495 to link the port city of Kabara with Timbuktu. Timbuktu was near enough to the Niger to take advantage of the commercial waterway, yet far enough to be beyond the river's area of seasonal inundation. Felix Dubois, *Timbuktu the Mysterious*, London, 1896.

Some African sovereigns attempted to boost urban revenue and stabilize prices by gaining control over the instruments of commercial exchange. In the fifteenth century Zanzibar's sultan minted his own metal coins, following the lead already taken by the neighboring city-state of Kilwa.[13] By the fifteenth century, many West African towns and cities had begun to use cowrie shells, mined mainly on Zanzibar Island and in the Maldive Islands of the Indian Ocean, as one form of currency. It was difficult to control the quantity and extent of their circulation. Cowrie shells in West Africa usually circulated in the large market towns. Elsewhere, the barter system generally prevailed. However, the king of the Kongo designated local, though rare, Nzimbu shells as the national currency and controlled their circulation by securing a royal monopoly over their source on the coast.[14]

Other forms of African currency included gold dust (Mwenemutapa empire, the East African coastal city-states, Ghana, Mali, Asante) salt blocks (Ethiopia, western Sudan, Saharan towns), copper ingots, bangles and bars (Mwenemutapa), iron manillas (West African coastal towns), and pieces of cloth (over a wide area). Even in African urban areas, barter persisted to a certain extent, the prices for most goods and services arrived at through time-consuming haggling between buyer and seller. Haggling resulted in part from the absence of a fixed set of weights and measures. To overcome this lack, the Askia Muhammad Touré of Songhay in about 1495 unified the system of weights and measures throughout the major towns and cities. He also appointed market inspectors to check against cheating or fraud.[15] This was an almost unprecedented act, for in most African markets considerable energy was consumed between individual buyers and sellers in reaching an equitable price.

Manners and Life Style

Revenues were used by urban rulers to support an elaborate court etiquette and life style. In the court of Benin city in 1553 aristocrats were forbidden to look directly at the king, and had to stare at the ground until instructed to do otherwise. Turning one's back to the monarch was not permitted, rendering it necessary to stride backward out of the audience chamber.[16] A similar procedure was found in the courts of the Ghanaian capital city of Kumbi-Saleh in the eleventh century. A North African visitor reported, "The governor of the city sits on the ground before the king and around him ministers seated likewise. . . . The audience is announced by the beating of a drum. . . . The people . . . fall on their knees and sprinkle dust on their heads for this is their way of showing respect for him."[17] In the kingdom of Kongo the rules of courtesy reflected subtle distinctions within the social and political hierarchy. A nineteenth-century description revealed that

> In a gathering of chiefs . . . the most important of the dignitaries grasps his own right wrist in his left hand, places the index finger of his right hand on the ground, carries it to his temples three times, opens the hand, presses the tips of the fingers to the ground, and then with closed fists beats the hands together rhythmically. This last gesture is repeated by every person present.[18]

Such procedures of etiquette may seem rather nonsensical to the modern eye. Yet they endowed urban rulers with a mystical aura which humbled even the most ambitious challenger of the status quo. In precolonial Africa, the secrets of leadership were obscured not only through architectural forms (chambers, walls, gates, etc.) but by complicated sets of manners. Rules of conduct also extended down through the social strata and gave community living an essential civility so lacking in contemporary areas of compressed humanity. On many streets of traditional Africa one would fall to his knees when greeting an older person, in order to show respect. And almost everywhere, youths would take off their sandals as they walked in front of the compound of an elder or chief.

The drive for prestige, more common to urban areas, was expressed by ostentatiously visible and audible accumulation of ornament. Early visitors to the great cities of Africa noted a vast and colorful array of clothing styles, jewelry, and hairdresses. In Abomey, an observer found that the rich dressed in cotton garments of European or local manufacture. The king and his ministers wore gold and silver-laced plumed hats while warriors dressed in grass loincloths made of the skin of palm-tree leaves, parted into small threads, knotted, and woven. Women adorned themselves with cowries and beads, metal rings, and coral-beaded earrings. Cloth was woven on local looms, and the dyes, especially the blue dyes, were "inferior to none."[19] Another visitor added that the wives of the king of Dahomey "were rather loaded than adorned with Gold Necklaces, Pendants, and Bracelets, Foot-Chains of Gold and Silver, and the richest Jewels."[20]

Even before European trade, urbanites in the Kongo dressed in high fashion. An early European traveler wrote:

> In ancient times the king and his courtiers . . . wore garments made from the palm-tree, which hung from the girdle downwards, and were fastened with belts of the same material, of beautiful workmanship. In front also, they wore as an ornament, and made like an apron, delicate skins of civet cats, martens, and sables, and also by way of display, a cape on the shoulders. Next the bare skin was a circular garment, somewhat like a rochet, reaching to the knees, and made like a net, from the threads of fine palm-tree cloths. . . . They threw back (the rochets) on the right shoulder . . . on the same shoulder carried a zebra's tail. . . . They wore very small yellow and red caps, square at the top, which scarcely covered the head, and were used more for show than as a protection from the sun or atmosphere. . . . [P]eople went barefoot, but the king and some of his nobles wore sandals. The poorer sort and common people wore the same kind of garments . . . but of a coarser cloth (they were naked from the waist up).[21]

A European in Kumasi in 1817 was surprised by the sight of the Muslims wearing "large cloaks of white satin, richly trimmed with spangled embroidery, their shirts and trowsers were of silk. . . ."[22] Around 1700 in Benin city, a visitor was struck by the elaborate hair arrangements: "the womens' Hair is very artificially curled-up in great and small Buckles, and divided on the Crown, like a Cock's Comb inverted, by which Means the small Curls lie in exact Order." He added, "Some divide their Hair into twenty or more Curls, as it happens to be thick or thin; others oil it with Palm Oil: By this Means its black Colour turns, in Time, to a sort of Green or Yellow, which they are very fond of. . . ."[23]

The Urban Arts

Much of the revenue collected by urban elites was used to patronize the guilds of artisans, which were usually physically attached to or in some way closely affiliated with the palace or the compounds of leading chiefs. The urban arts may have reached their peak of stylization, diversity, and articulation in the artisan's workshops of Benin city in the mid- to late fifteenth century. In Benin there were well-organized guilds of brassworkers, blacksmiths, carpenters, weavers, leatherworkers, wood carvers, and potters. The domestic arts, which included wood carving, probably started in the reign of Ere (*ca.* A.D. 900–980) when wooden heads were carved and placed on ancestral shrines.[24] According to oral history, the technique of lost-wax casting in copper alloys was introduced to the rulers of Benin city by Ife artisans some time around A.D. 1250 to 1350.[25] This art may have begun at Ife as early as the ninth century and there reached its peak of delicate naturalism. The heads or masks cast in metal at Ife and Benin were probably of a commemorative or memorial nature, in honor of

72. Tano shrine house, built in the Asante Union on the eve of the European conquest. Such shrines are noteworthy for the superb architectural qualities. Note the sculptured facade. Author's photo.

deceased kings or queen mothers. Later, at Benin, bronze plaques of a commemorative and decorative purpose were cast to adorn the pillars in the galleries of the Oba's palace. On the plaques, kings, chiefs, and warriors were portrayed in elaborate costumes with weapons and attendants. While the casting of plaques ceased around the end of the seventeenth century, Benin artisans continued to turn out a rich array of bronze cocks, crocodiles, rams, leopards, and other animals. Efforts were made to keep the lost-wax process a state secret, reserved for the palace guilds. But in time artisans in other towns learned the

73. Benin. Bronze plaque with chief (*left*) and two
attendants (late sixteenth or early seventeenth century). William Basom, *African Art in Cultural Per-
spective*, W. W. Norton, © 1973.

technique. Nevertheless, for the most part it remained an art form of
the rich and privileged. In Benin, the use of ivory was also a royal
prerogative; and Obas would wear intricately carved ivory armlets,
which helped to distinguish them from their handsomely dressed
palace retainers.

In precolonial Yoruba and Ibo towns, artisans produced wooden
door panels displaying designs or narrative scenes carved in relief.
They were used in shrines and to decorate the houses of wealthy
families. Yoruba panels were alive with human and animal figures,
while those of the Ibo were of pleasing geometric designs. Nearby in
the city-states of the Niger Delta, memorial screens adorned assembly

halls to commemorate prominent ancestors. Yoruba towns were also known for their weavers, resist-cloth dyers, tailors, and manufacturers of musical instruments.

Kumasi was famous for its goldsmiths, who turned out fine jewelry, and for its weavers of Kente cloth, a woven material of rich blue, gold, and red worn by the wealthy families on ceremonial occasions. Each Kente pattern had a name and associated proverb. It is said that the art of weaving Kente was brought to Kumasi in 1723 after Asante's victory over neighboring Techiman and the exile of its artisans to Kumasi.[26]

Kumasi and surrounding Asante towns were also famous for the manufacture of brass weights, used for measuring gold dust, a major currency. The weights portrayed human and animal figures in their daily lives and referred to proverbial expressions. This form is of considerable antiquity, for Europeans mention it as far back as 1602. It was also in Kumasi that the famous wooden state stools were carved and decorated with silver or gold sheeting. The golden stool of the Asantehenes, or kings, dates to at least the late seventeenth century with the commencement of the reign of Osei Tutu, founder of the Asante nation.

74. A chief's dwelling near Lake Albert in East Africa. Note the elaborate portals.

Artisans at Abomey, capital of Dahomey, fabricated colorful tapestries with appliqué patterns depicting important historical events and achievements in the lives of the various kings. These tapestries graced the walls of the palaces at Abomey and served to add legitimacy to the ruling dynasty. Herskovits noted, "This dependence upon the king of the artists . . . determined their place in Dahomean society, so that they were essentially courtiers in position, affiliation, and loyalties to the monarch." He added, "The groups which did this work were not numerous, and geographically they were and are confined to Abomey."[27] These artisans, all men, lived in a series of compounds near the royal palace; and all appliqué cloths were made by them alone.

In Hausaland, one of the most distinctive urban crafts was embroidery. Heathcote observed, "Extensive hand embroidery being something of a luxury, the important customers would originally have been the rulers, their courtiers, and the wealthy traders. It is, therefore, in those important political and trading cities where a sarki (chief) would have had a large retinue, that we could expect to have found the greatest number of embroiderers."[28]

Cities of the western Sudan also boasted of expert embroiderers, as well as numerous tailors. In Timbuktu alone, there were at least twenty-six tailors' shops, each of which employed between fifty and one hundred apprentices. Although linen and cotton cloth was woven in Timbuktu, large quantities of fabric were imported from Europe via the Barbary Coast of North Africa.[29]

In the city-states of the East African coast, cloth weaving became at an early date one of the most important industries. The gold of Sofala's markets was paid for in part in fine cloth, most of which was manufactured at Kilwa. Swahili urbanites were famous throughout the western Indian Ocean for their elegant flowing gowns. Equally famous were the magnificently carved doors which graced the entryways of aristocratic homes.

At Great Zimbabwe, in the interior, there is little evidence of organized craft guilds. However, craftsmen did turn out engraved monoliths and birds made of soft dark-green soapstone. Soapstone, though plentiful in the Mwenemutapan empire, was apparently carved only at Great Zimbabwe. In addition, there was fine ceramic pottery, clay animal figurines, and a wide variety of iron implements of excellent workmanship. Craftsmen also fashioned gold and copper wire into bracelets for wrists, forearms, ankles, and calves.

Education

Scant information exists on the development of education in precolonial African towns and cities, with the exception of those under Muslim leadership. Preliterate urban centers had a very limited formal educational apparatus. Most urbanites acquired learning through direct, face-to-face contacts. Youths learned from family members in their compound or from firsthand experience in the streets, marketplace, or at work. Public information was diffused by troubadors, street-singers, dancers, actors, or story-tellers. Often, each quarter would contain a guild of town criers who transmitted official news from the central administration to their own people. Every ruling urban dynasty had attached to its family a *griot*, or raconteur, whose responsibility it was to relate orally to the masses the major historical events in the life of the city and the accomplishments of prominent individuals. However, every institution, from family lineages to guilds, had its own oral reciters, who conveyed information relating to the historical experience of their particular group. On ceremonial occasions, they would recount, often for money, this information. Often they would speak to the accompaniment of drummers, buglers, and flutists. Through the *griot*, the lower classes were made to grasp the norms that governed the social, economic, and political order. For all residents, they gave the city an essential sense of historical continuity and *raison d'être*.

For the masses, the major centers of education were the marketplace, community wells, and the ceremonial or parade ground in front of the palace. Education for the aristocrats took place within the compounds of kings and paramount chiefs. George Balandier in his study of the Kongo discovered that "Boys belonging to noble families were sent to the *mbanza* (capital towns), where they learned suitable manners and military arts, and were introduced to public affairs through the numerous services they rendered."[30] This pattern was repeated elsewhere in precolonial African kingdoms. Within a local chief's compound, youths were instructed in manners and behavior toward their elders and in the proper ways of addressing the king and other members of the hierarchy and nobility. Those who were outstanding were sent to the king's residence, where they joined other youths from throughout the kingdom for more intensive training. Students showing an aptitude as potential warriors were given military posts, and those who possessed talents of political leadership were admitted into the civil service.

Whenever Islam entered African society, it tended to add a deeper and wider dimension to education. With Islam came the written word; and writing paved the way for the broader dissemination and greater accumulation of knowledge. Formal, structured education became more prevalent, especially in the great centers of trans-Saharan and trans-Indian Ocean trade.

From about the twelfth century, small Qur'anic schools blossomed within Islamic quarters of Sudanic cities. As trade between tropical Africa and the Muslim world increased, the number of Qur'anic schools grew. Gradually, Islamic education became entrenched and indigenized in the major market towns. Islam enriched traditional learning by exposing it to intellectual currents in the expansive and cosmopolitan Muslim world. Qur'anic scholarship throughout Africa followed routes of Muslim trade and immigration. From the eleventh century, Arab geographers alluded to the existence of Islamic scholars in the important market towns of ancient Ghana. Eastward, in the fledgling Niger River city of Gao, the king received a Qur'an upon his conversion to Islam in A.D. 1010. While this gift may indicate his own literacy, there is nothing to suggest that Islamic learning had extended much beyond Gao's royal compounds and central marketplace. The ruler of Bornu also embraced the faith in the eleventh century. Yet scant evidence exists for the presence of large numbers of clerics. A similar commentary could be made for the East African coast, where Islamic learning from the thirteenth to the nineteenth century remained within the confines of the city-states.

Islamic education was given a great boost in the cities of the Mali empire when Mansa Musa returned from his Meccan pilgrimage in 1325 with many Muslim scholars. In the late fifteenth century and early sixteenth century the Askia Muhammad Touré of Songhay gave Islamic learning further encouragement. The Askia had grown rich on the trans-Saharan trade and by accumulating booty from his wars of territorial expansion. Much of this wealth was lavished on the Muslim *ulama* (scholars) in the intellectual cities of Djenné, Tim-

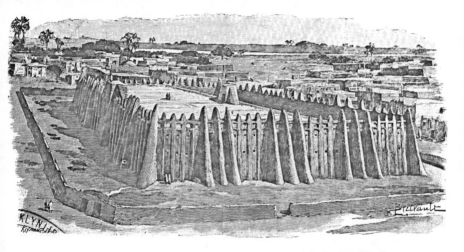

75. The old mosque at Timbuktu. Timbuktu was one of the leading Muslim centers of learning in the Western Sudan between the fourteenth and sixteenth centuries. The growth of Timbuktu and Djenné as important centers of Islamic learning occurred alongside their development as commercial cities. Felix Dubois, *Timbouctou le Mystérieux*, Paris, 1896.

buktu, and Gao. The number of Qur'anic schools in Djenné multiplied, and the prestigious Sankore mosque at Timbuktu flowered into an important center for Islamic studies. Scholars throughout the Muslim world of North Africa and the Middle East traveled in the sixteenth century to Timbuktu's 180 schools for instruction and teaching. In the bustling markets, teachers bargained with traders for books and writing paper imported from North Africa. Songhay's Muslim scholars served as vital advisors to the Askias and were rewarded with slaves, food, property, books, and other treasures. The Askias encouraged the scholars to use this wealth for pilgrimages to Mecca and other leading centers of North Africa and Egypt.

Islamic education received an infusion in the Bornu empire under Mai Idris Alooma in 1570–1610. Through his sponsorship a continuous flow of scholars was maintained with Bornu, Tripoli, and Egypt. Hostels for Bornu scholars were elected and expanded in Cairo and on the outskirts of Mecca. In the nineteenth century, Islamic learning obtained its greatest forward thrust from militant teacher-statesmen in the broad savanna between the Niger and Senegal rivers and eastward in Hausaland. The *zakat* tithe, a social obligation among Muslims, was used in the Sudanic states for the benefit of the poor, scholars, and clerics. In the theocratic states in the nineteenth century, *zakat* became a compulsory tax levied by government officials.

Monumental Urban Architecture

Without substantial revenue, an educated elite, and a large labor force, it would have been impossible for a town or city to undertake the construction of public buildings on a monumental scale. That so little monumental architecture exists in sub-Saharan Africa is probably a reflection of the difficulty in accumulating the necessary wealth and labor, particularly in societies with underdeveloped monetary systems.

Because most peasants lived in noncentralized, politically segmented societies, most of their dwellings were refreshingly practical, serenely modest, and unobtrusive. They were simple enough to allow every African family, even the poorest and most lowly, a home of its own. The structures were usually simple enough to be built by the cooperative efforts of the extended family. Kongolese families went to the extreme of simplifying and speeding construction by prefabricating their buildings. Component sections were constructed separately and then transported to the site for assembly.

Monumental architecture, on the other hand, is often associated with foreign trade and/or political centralization. Kings were needed to corvee labor for the construction of massive public-works projects. Sultans, Emirs, and the like built big to overawe their subjects and to impress foreign visitors. The *Tarikh al Fettach* tells us that when Askia Muhammad Touré conquered Diaga in 1495 he captured five hundred masons and dispatched 80 percent of them to the city of Gao.[31] Indeed, it was in the reign of this Askia that the enormous mud-brick mosques of the major Sudanic cities of Songhay were constructed. Labelle Prussin is undoubtedly correct when she says, "The existence of Songhai-derived masonry castes over possible substrata of widespread Bambara technology may very well account for the development of a monumental architecture in the Niger bend, such as that of Jenné itself."[32]

Windham, when visiting Benin city in the sixteenth century, was overwhelmed by the size of the Oba's compound, which he estimated to be "as large as the town of Haarlem . . . and divided into many magnificent palaces, houses, and apartments . . . and comprises

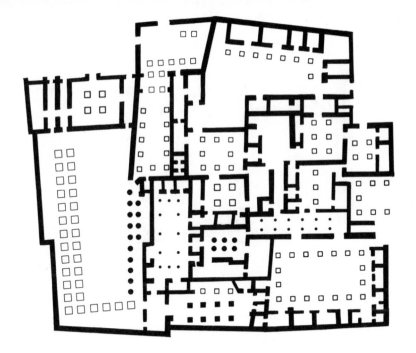

PLAN OF A YORUBA PALACE.

beautiful and long square galleries, about as large as the Exchange at Amsterdam."[33] Hugh Clapperton, on his travels through the city of Old Oyo in the early nineteenth century, estimated that the Alafin's palace (Afin) covered approximately 640 acres or one square mile.[34] Edward Bowdich in Kumasi described the Asantehene's palace as "an immense building of a variety of oblong courts and regular squares, the former with arcades along the one side, some of round arches symmetrically turned . . . the entablatures exuberantly adorned in bold fan and trellis work. . . ."[35]

On the East African coast at Kilwa, the Husuni Kubwa palace and trading emporium was the largest single building in sub-Saharan Africa at the time of its erection in about 1245. Made of enormous blocks of coral, with massive conical, fluted vaults and domes, it contained over one hundred rooms with courtyards, terraces, and a sunken swimming pool. Together with the Great Mosque (ca. 1270), it made Kilwa a city of great architectural merit. By 1331, Ibn Battuta could speak of it as "one of the most beautiful and well-constructed cities in the world. The whole of it is elegantly built."[36]

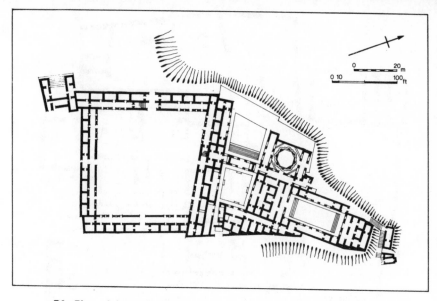

76. Plan of the early–fourteenth-century palace and trading emporium of Husuni Kubwa at Kilwa along the East African coast. Chambers are situated around rectangular courtyards and an octagonal pool. Courtesy Thames and Hudson, *Great Zimbabwe*, P. S. Garlake, © 1973.

Deep in the interior reposed the architectural gems of Great Zimbabwe. Peter Garlake has called the walled Great Enclosure "the largest single prehistoric structure in sub-Saharan Africa."[37] Equally impressive is the mysterious Conical Tower, built in the finest stone masonry style. The overall scale and precision of the cut-stone structures of Great Zimbabwe are without parallel on the subcontinent.

Decline and Deterioration

Environment can influence urbanization by imposing limits upon city growth. Likewise, towns and cities have vanished as a result of shifting environmental circumstances or of the overutilization of vital natural resources. Kimbi-Saleh, capital of the Ghanaian empire, was described in about 1067 as a city abounding in wells of sweet water, which were used to cultivate lush green vegetable gardens.[38] Today, the city lies in ruins in a semi-desert waste. Some ecologists believe that overgrazing and famine brought on by the southward march of the Sahara were important factors in the city's demise. By the time of the Almoravid invasion in 1076 Kumbi-Saleh's large population was probably already hard pressed for food and water.

Environmental deterioration may also account for the decline of Great Zimbabwe. Peter Garlake suggests that the ecological characteristics of the territory surrounding Great Zimbabwe could not support a large population. Major factors in the city's decline, he says, were overgrazing, soil exhaustion, excessive logging of the surrounding forests, and depletion of wild game. To compound the dilemma, in the mid-fifteenth century the city suffered a shortage of salt, which was an essential item of diet. Disruptions of trade at that time may have triggered this salt crisis. In any case, Great Zimbabwe declined rather swiftly over the following three or four decades.[39]

Thaba Bosiu, city of refuge and capital of the Kingdom of Basutoland, was also affected by environmental deterioration. Located on top of a small plateau, it was protected enough to resist attacks from land-hungry Boers of the Orange Free State but too small to support a burgeoning population. Ultimately, the residents of Thaba Bosiu were unable to endure overcrowding, shortages of water, rinderpest

77. Conical tower in the Great Enclosure of Great Zimbabwe. It is thirty-four feet high and constructed of cut stone without the use of mortar. It may have been used for religious purposes. Author's photo.

epizootics, and famine. King Moshweshwe's successors abandoned the city, and today it is little more than a rocky, barren ruin.

While environment was a critical factor in the destiny of many African towns and cities, still more urban centers floundered with the collapse of their political superstructures. Timbuktu, Djenné, and Gao declined rapidly after the political collapse of the Songhay empire in the wake of the Moroccan invasion of 1591. Likewise, Old Oyo began to disintegrate when the leading state officials and military officers repudiated the Alafin's (king's) authority after he had unconstitutionally attacked a dependency of the sacred city of Ife in 1793. Political instability and economic dislocation became so great that many people began to desert the city and move southward. Finally, when the elaborate political apparatus was withdrawn from Old Oyo following the Fulani invasion in 1837, the city disappeared altogether.

Cities on the fringes of empire may at times break away from the metropolis and become the bases of operation for attacks on the mother city. Kumasi, economic and political nerve center of the Asante confederacy, is a case in point. The British bombardment of the city in 1874 weakened the central government and state army. Provincial capitals—Kokofu, Bekwai, Dwaben, and Mampong—soon broke away and challenged the authority of Kumasi's governing institutions. Fortunately, the magnetic pull of the Golden Stool, the symbol of Asante national unity, which resided in Kumasi, proved irresistible in the end and Kumasi survived as capital city. The city endured, despite periodic foreign and domestic threats, because of its symbolic value for all Asante people. Other cities in Africa, particularly those of a purely commercial or political nature, succumbed to similar challenges.

External military invasions may bring utter destruction indeed to urban centers. In 1895, the armies of Samory Touré invaded the ancient Niger River city of Kong and burned it to the ground. In the space of a few hours one of the greatest commercial, political, and intellectual cities of West Africa passed into oblivion. On the East African coast, Portuguese attacks on Sofala, Kilwa, Zanzibar, and Mombasa between 1502 and 1505 laid waste the markets of these once-flourishing city-states.[40] They would not recover until the heyday of Sultan Sayyid Said in the fourth decade of the nineteenth

78. Panorama of the city of Kong, a savanna city founded by Senufo which lay north of the modern Ivory Coast in a region famous for the production of kola nuts. Mande Dyula traders began to settle in the city, and by 1730 had transformed it into one of West Africa's most active Islamic and market centers and the capital of a small federal state. By 1888 it had a multi-ethnic population of over 15,000. Kong's chief industries were basket-making, weaving, and cloth dyeing. Its Sudanic-style mosques were adorned by double pyramidal minarets. The armies of Samory attacked and completely destroyed the city in 1895. L. G. Binger, *Voyage du Niger au Golfe de Guinée*, Paris, 1888.

century. Actually, Sofala never recovered, because its trade routes to the gold and copper mines of the interior were severed.

Although towns and cities usually floundered with the weakening or collapse of their political superstructures, some stood the chance of being perpetuated and even revived under a new order. European imperialists blasted their way into many African cities in the late nineteenth century only to rebuild them as colonial metropolises in the twentieth. Kumasi, Kano, Ibadan, Mombasa, Zanzibar, Kampala, and many other historic cities experienced new vitality during the colonial period. With independence, the destiny of these cities has again returned to African leadership. And they have become the economic cornerstones of flourishing modernizing economies.

[1] Adu Boahen, *Topics in West African History* (London, 1966), p. 8.

[2] Nehemiah Levtzion, *Ancient Ghana and Mali* (London, 1973), p. 157.

[3] H. A. S. Johnston, *The Fulani Empire of Sokoto* (London, 1967), p. 9.

[4] Oral testimony, Mallam Urwatu, Katsina, 4 July 1966.

[5] Archibald Dalzel, *The History of Dahomey* (1793; reprinted London 1963), p. xii.

[6] K. O. Dike, *Trade and Politics in the Niger Delta, 1830–1885* (London, 1956), p. 29.

[7] Jan Vansina, *Kingdoms of the Savanna* (Madison, Wis., 1968), p. 44.

[8] Ivor Wilks, "Ashanti Government," in Daryll Forde and P. M. Kaberry, eds., *West African Kingdoms in the Nineteenth Century* (London, 1967), p. 215.

[9] J. Lombard, "The Kingdom of Dahomey," *Ibid.*, p. 71.

[10] Willem Bosman, A *New and Accurate Description of the Coast of Guinea . . .* (London, 1705), p. 462.

[11] T. Edward Bowdich, *Mission From Cape Coast Castle to Ashantee* (London, 1819), p. 295.

[12] H. Ling Roth, *Great Benin* (1903, reprinted New York, 1968), p. 109. Captain J. F. Landolphe, who visited Benin in 1778, noted that all visitors had to have their feet washed before entering the city.

[13] See G. S. P. Freeman-Grenville, *Medieval History of the Tanganyika Coast* (London, 1962).

[14] Jan Vansina, *Kingdoms of the Savanna.* p. 44. Vansina notes that "the income was used to grant gifts to the titleholders at court and sometimes to territorial rulers, for only through gifts could the kings hope to retain an impressive retinue of officials, soldiers, pages, musicians, etc., at court."

[15] Adu Boahen, *Topics in West African History*, p. 29.

[16] Roth, *Great Benin*, p. 107.

[17] A. Boahen, "Kingdoms of West Africa," in Boahen, ed., *Horizon History of Africa* (New York, 1971), p. 182.

[18] Georges Balandier, *Daily Life in the Kingdom of the Kongo* (London, 1968), p. 177.

[19] Dalzel, *History of Dahomey*, pp. xxiv, xvii.

[20] Thomas Astley, A *New and General Collection of Voyages and Travels* (London, 1745), 3:43.

[21] Filippo Pigafetta, A *Report of the Kingdom of Congo* (1591), M. Hutchinson, trans. (New York, 1969), p. 108.

[22] Bowdich, *Mission From Cape Coast Castle*, p. 37.

[23] Nyendael in Astley, A *New and General Collection*, 3:96.

[24] Philip J. C. Dark, An *Introduction to Benin Art and Technology* (Oxford, 1973), p. 6.

[25] Frank Willett, *Ife in the History of West African Sulpture* (New York, 1967), pp. 52–57.

26 Dennis M. Warren, "Bono Royal Regalia," *African Arts* 8, no. 2 (1975): 16.

27 Melville Herskovits, *Dahomey: An Ancient West African Kingdom*, vol. 2 (New York, 1938):315.

28 David Heathcote, "Hausa Embroidered Dress," *African Arts* 5, no. 2 (1972): 13.

29 Levtzion, *Ancient Ghana and Mali*, p. 120.

30 Balandier, *Daily Life in the Kingdom of the Kongo*, p. 225.

31 Labelle Prussin, "Sudanese Architecture and the Manding," *African Arts* 3, no. 4 (1970): 64. The central mosque at Djenné was also expanded and soon took on the appearance of an enormous block, rigidly square with sides measuring 183 feet long by 39 feet high. See Felix DuBois, *Timbucktoo the Mysterious* (London, 1896), p. 156.

32 Prussin, "Sudanese Architecture," 64.

33 Roth, *Great Benin*. p. 160.

34 Hugh Clapperton, *Journal of A Second Expedition into the Interior of Africa* (London, 1829), p. 58. In the Kingdom of Kongo, the Mani Kongo's palace was said to have spread over one square mile (see Hakluyt Soc. Vol. 1 1896. p. 73). Smith noted in 1724 that the palace of the king of Dahomey was almost one and a half miles in circumference (see William Smith, *A New Voyage to Guinea* [1744] [New York, 1967], p. 173).

35 Bowdich from Freda Wolfson, ed., *Pageant of Ghana* (London, 1958), pp. 105–6.

36 Peter S. Garlake, *The Early Islamic Architecture of the East African Coast* (Nairobi, 1966), p. 27. The utilization of mortar permitted the construction of arches and vaults and thus gave a monumentality to numerous structures.

37 Garlake, *Early Islamic Architecture*. p. 29.

38 Levtzion, *Ancient Ghana and Mali*. p. 23.

39 Peter S. Garlake, *Great Zimbabwe* (London, 1973), p. 198.

40 Justus Strandes, *The Portuguese Period in East Africa* (1899; reprinted Nairobi, 1961), pp. 38–54, 66–81, 117–29.

SUMMARY

THERE is a tendency to assume that urban life in Africa is exclusively the outcome of European contact, European stimulus to trade and commercial development, and the European imposition of Western urban values. The foregoing chapters have attempted to reveal that African towns and cities antedated European conquest and domination and that many urban centers played an important role in the advancement of African civilization.

Compelling evidence of urban life dates deep into African antiquity. The iron-working industrial city of Meroë rose on the banks of the upper Nile in 593 B.C.; and foundations for the spiritual city of Ife in West Africa were laid sometime between the sixth and ninth centuries A.D. Almost contemporaneous was the emergence of the East African city-states, Great Zimbabwe in Central Africa, and the great urban emporiums of the western and central Sudan. One could dwell at length on the antiquity of African towns and cities. But the point is that urban living is neither a new nor an alien phenomenon in Africa south of the Sahara.

African towns and cities may be defined in part by their major purpose. There were spiritual and ceremonial cities like Ife and Daura whose *raison d'être* derived from their respective positions as fonts of Yoruba and Hausa civilization. There were also the commercial centers of exchange. Cities of the West African Sudan mushroomed from the expansion of trade between the southern forests and North Africa and Egypt. Similarly, the Swahili city-states sprang from trade between Arabia, Persia, India and the East and Central African hinterland; and in like manner towns and cities of the West African forests flourished as conduits for goods flowing between the southern savanna and forest and the Atlantic coast. Other cities served primarily as centers of governance, such as the Kongolese *mbanza* (political center) the seat of the *mani* (king), or the *kibuga*, capital of Buganda's *kabakas* or divine rulers. The destinies of these cities were inextricably linked to the ruler's tenure in office. Indeed, cities and rulers rose and fell together. Equally tenuous were the cities of refuge, notably Moshweshwe's Thaba Bosiu in southern Africa, Mkwana's Kalenga in East Africa, Bida city in the Nupe region of Nigeria, and the stockaded towns of Sierra Leone. Inevitably, the restoration of peace and security from wars and slave-raiding led to a decline in their residential populations. However, refugee towns such as Ibadan, which developed commerce and craft industries, prospered and endured. Finally, there were the cities of vision, of almost utopian purpose. Freetown, Monrovia, and Libreville resulted from attempts at black Christian social and economic regeneration. Sokoto, another act of will, was created as a spiritual and political center for the rejuvenation of Islam, while Kukawa in neighboring Bornu was built to symbolize Al-Kanami's triumph over the reactionary forces of the Sefawa dynasty and as a bold assertion of a new political order.

Thus, African towns and cities served a number of purposes and functions, most of them exhibited a combination of two or more of them. Kumasi and Benin acted simultaneously as political, spiritual, commercial, and artistic capitals of their respective Asante and Edo peoples. Great Zimbabwe became first a ritual center, then a political and commercial nucleus of the Rozwi. Abomey won world attention as political, artistic, and cultic focal point of the Fon peoples.

It is therefore incorrect to view precolonial African urban centers as purely the outgrowth of responses to European stimuli. Nor can we establish that markets or commercial and industrial activity are prerequisites for the existence of towns and cities. Some urban centers, particularly Ife and the *kibugas* of Buganda, spurned the commercial ethic yet became prototypes, from a morphological point of view, for other communities. Even in the great commercial cities, manufacturing was a small-scale operation, confined to family compounds and the marketplace. Nearly everywhere, part-time agriculturalists constituted a sizable, though seldom dominating, proportion of the urban population.

II.

Another major misconception about precolonial Africans is that their settlement patterns were a disorganized, cacophonous, sprawling scramble of random structures, exhibiting little or no regard for the elements of rational planning. Oral and written evidence reveals the importance of human relationships as a major determinant in the placement of buildings. They also suggest that the utilization of space was hardly haphazard. Nevertheless, it was not space that mattered so much as the relationships of its occupants. Space was seen as a medium in which to express relationships of a social, religious, ethnic, political, or occupational nature. Thus, urban compounds were arranged spatially on the basis of the hierarchies of their residents. Kinship and lineage structures were reinforced by the compartmentalization of urban space. Although mobility was stifled, the beneficial role of the family as an educative, acculturative, cooperative labor and welfare mechanism was greatly enhanced. This attention to human relationships over geometric considerations undoubtedly helped to minimize criminality, social disorientation, and anomie.

Many towns and cities held a clear conception of the importance of the "center." This was perhaps most vividly expressed in the radial-concentric Yoruba and Hausa cities of Nigeria, where all roads led, like spokes of a great wheel, to the palace and adjacent marketplace. Compounds of provincial chiefs were situated at varying distances from the city center, depending on rank and social status.

Unlike contemporary African and Western megalopolises, with limitless, confusing suburbs, the preindustrial city was often clearly defined by earthenworks, in the form of ditches or walls of timber, mud, or stone. Walls gave urban containers an identity and its inhabitants a reassuring sense of security. Its gates, on the other hand, served as powerful instruments of coercion, controlling the movement of population and goods.

Towns and cities were characterized by tight compound clustering, though they were also broken by large expanses of public space. Major political capitals were intersected by broad, processional avenues,

which in Kumasi, for example, exceeded one hundred yards in width.
Typical also were sweeping parade grounds, rolling out before the
palace gates like a huge brown carpet. More than mere conveyors of
trade items and livestock, these great pedestrianways and gathering
points served also as vital lines of human communication, where
urban values, etiquette, and historic traditions were periodically acted
out and reaffirmed. They were great human stages upon which all
social and political strata visibly expressed their identity and purpose.
Street patterns in politically centralized, authoritarian communities
tended to be radial (Yoruba, Hausa) or on a modified grid (Loango,
Benin, Abomey, Kumasi), while in societies with more diffused
authority (Ibo) they were winding labyrinths. All of them, however,
were streets for people, not vehicles; and they exhibited a certain
vitality, humaneness and warmth lacking in the motorways of the
modern industrial cities of today.

III.

Most towns and cities were linked in some way to their immediate
hinterlands, at least to the extent of profiting from the countryside's
excess of food production. In cosmopolitan Muslim cities, ties with
their outlying non-Islamic villages were predominantly economic and
political; while in spiritually and ethnically homogeneous cities, such
as those of Yorubaland or Benin, the connections were more of a
socioreligious nature. In fact, the Yoruba regarded the countryside as
an extension of the town. Town-dwellers and ruralists in the Benin
and Oyo empires tended to share a common ethnic and religious
background; moreover, many urban residents commuted regularly to
their suburban farms. Yoruba towns practiced a symbiotic relationship with their rural relatives. By contrast, city-states along the East
African coast were in an essentially predatory position vis-à-vis their
hinterlands, particularly with the growth of the slave and ivory trade
fostered by the Sultan Said in the mid-nineteenth century. In many
areas of Africa, the nobility maintained land and compounds in the
surrounding countryside. Yet by the nineteenth century, there was a
tendency for them to become absentee landlords, living at the capital
and delegating tax-collecting and administrative responsibilities to
their titled slaves. Political capitals were often microcosms of the
entire realm. Consequently, it was not unusual to find them divided

into numerous sections corresponding to the outlying provinces and occupied by peoples from that particular area. In this way, all urbanites originating in a given rural province or chieftaincy were kept together in one quarter or ward of the city.

IV.

Europeans and Americans have long held the image of African habitations as structurally unsophisticated and monotonous in design. This study has attempted to correct that stereotype by revealing the diversity of form, design, and function in traditional African architecture. Precolonial African towns and cities exhibited a seemingly infinite variety of forms, rising from the basic circular, square, or rectangular foundation. They included a multitude of variations on such forms as the bullet, onion, beehive, complete cone or cone-on-cylinder; the steeple-crowned square or cylinder; the clay rectangular or square box under a flat, vaulted, or domical roof; the termite-hill–type tower with porcupine exterior; the rectangular box with gable-ended roof; and so on. Towns and cities themselves were often mosaics of building forms; and these basic forms were constructed with a wide variety of building materials, including stone, coral block, bulk mud or clay, mud-brick, clapboard, reed, grass thatch, palm frond, and leaves, to mention only a few of the most common materials.

African architecture was constantly changing because of the comparative impermanence of building materials. Next to grass, clay was probably the most common material. The explanation lies in Africa's abundance of red lateritic soil, which possesses a high clay content. Exceptionally plastic, clay and mud also act as good insulators and retainers of heat. Their plasticity allows the artisan-builder wide latitude in working interesting wall designs in bold relief.

Occupations exerted a strong influence on architectural form and technique. In some areas fascinating comparisions can be drawn between home building and basket making or, in Dogon country, between house form and the design and shape of ceremonial dance masks. Changes in building technique, style, and form were frequently a good indication of transition occurring within society itself. Foreign influences in political, social, and religious belief systems led to variations on old themes or totally new architectonic departures.

Shifts from nomadic pastoralism to sedentary agriculture resulted in greater utilization of bulk-mud and mud-brick than thatch and light woods, which were more mobile. And with Islam came strong emphasis on square and rectangular forms.

Thus, many factors influenced the habitations of precolonial Africa, though none were as important as the natural environment, specifically climate, soil, and vegetation. It is not surprising that African architecture was distinguished by its adaptability to the natural setting. Structures often blended into the environment, achieving a synthesis of vernacular and organic forms. Great Zimbabwe's stonework simulated preexisting boulders or became extensions of them. Early Ethiopian churches were chiseled out of solid bedrock like pieces of sculpture. Whole communities mirrored their surrounding countryside and acted as a kind of human camouflage. The tan-colored Sudanic cities seemed almost to merge into the natural sun-scorched surroundings, while the grassy and leaflike dwellings of the high savanna and forest appeared to be natural extensions of the encompassing undergrowth. The coral mosques, tombs, and merchants' houses in the Swahili cities echoed the sparkling coral-studded

79. Dogon village (Mali). Photo: Carole Howard.

80. Residential mud compounds (Katsina city, northern Nigeria). Author's photo.

shoreline. Everywhere, African towns and cities seemed to be in dynamic complementarity with the natural landscape.

V.

In conclusion, it must be emphasized that Africans possess an architectural heritage of their own; and that they can profess to preindustrial urban cultures worthy of comparison with any urban civilizations of the world. To grasp space; to know how to use it; to see a potential unity among edifice, ethos, and environment; and to perceive a synthesis of form and function are the crucial criteria for urban excellence. Precolonial African architecture displayed a clear recognition of these elements.

African architecture and urban design obtained considerable inspiration and initial impetus from the creative intelligence of indigenous peoples. Doubtless, there were some external influences: Ethiopian ecclesiastical architecture was influenced by Byzantium; East African coastal designs drew inspiration from the Arabian peninsula, Persia, western India, and elsewhere; Sudanic styles were reminiscent of the Muslim Middle East, Egypt, and North Africa; and some West African coastal towns reflected styles found in pre-Columbian Europe. But for the most part, African architecture and urban design were rooted in the religious, political, economic, and social conceptions of the local populace.

African towns and cities were at once utilitarian, ornamental, and humane. They symbolized not only man's relationship to his fellow man and the cosmos but man's adaptation to the natural environment. Rather than conquer and destroy nature, the African builder revered and complemented it. Moreover, urban living radiated a spirit of mutual aid and cooperation, of civility and gentility, of good manners and etiquette. There was a sensitive interrelatedness to everything; and it was that quality that made African towns and cities, and the structures within them, works of art.

BIBLIOGRAPHY

I. Primary Sources, Including Unpublished Manuscripts

AFRICANUS, LEO. *The History and Description of Africa.* Vol. 1, London (Hakluyt), 1896.

AMEYAW, ADU G. "Ashanti Traditional Religious Architecture." M. S. thesis, Kumasi, 1967.

ASTLEY, THOMAS. A *New and General Collection of Voyages and Travels.* London, 1745.

BARTH, HENRY. *Travels and Discoveries in North and Central Africa.* Vol. 1. New York, 1857.

BOSMAN, WILLEM. A *New and Accurate Description of the Coast of Guinea.* 1705; reprinted New York, 1968.

BOVILL, E . W., ed. *Missions to the Niger.* Vols. 1–4. Cambridge, 1966.

BOWDICH, T. EDWARD. *Mission From Cape Coast Castle to Ashantee.* London, 1819.

BURTON, RICHARD F. *Mission to Gelele, King of Dahomey.* Vol. 1. 1864; London, 1893 edition.

CLAPPERTON, HUGH. *Journal of a Second Expedition into the Interior of Africa.* 1829; reprinted New York, 1966.

CRONE, G. R. *The Voyages of Cadamosto* London (Hakluyt), 1937.

DALZEL, ARCHIBALD. *The History of Dahomey.* 1793; reprinted London, 1963.

DAMES, M. L., trans. *The Book of Duarte Barbosa.* 1518; reprinted New York, 1967.

EFFAH, EMMANUEL. "Pedestrians in Kumasi City Centre." M. S. thesis, Kumasi 1967.

EGHAREVBA, JACOB. A *Short History of Benin.* 1934; reprinted Ibadan, 1960.

ENGESTROM, TOR. "Origin of Pre-Islamic Architecture in West Africa," *Ethnos* 24, no. 2 (1959).

EQUIANO, OLAUDAH. *Narrative of the Life of Olaudah Equiano.* London, 1789.

FERGUSON, PHYLLIS. "Mosques and the Islamization Process in the 19th Century among the Eastern Dyula." unpublished ms., 1971.

FRAIKU, I. K. "Elmina House Types from 1400 to 1899." M. S. thesis, Kumasi, 1965.

FREEMAN, R. A. *Travels and Life in Ashanti and Jaman.* London, 1898.

HERSKOVITS, MELVILLE. *Dahomey: An Ancient West African Kingdom.*

2 vols. New York, 1938.

JANZEN, JOHN M. "The Manianga Architecture of Process: A Study of Form and Space in Northern Kongo." unpubl. ms., 1970.

JOHNSON, SAMUEL. *The History of the Yorubas*, London, 1921; reprinted 1969.

JOHNSTON, HARRY. *George Grenfell and the Congo*. Vol. 2. 1908; reprinted New York, 1969.

KOFI, S. G. T. "Traditional Architecture of Ghana." M. S. thesis, Kumasi, 1965.

MALLAM URWATU. Oral testimony. Katsina 4 July 1966.

MASINBO, VICTOR K. O. "Chief Nwokeji's Compound." M. S. thesis, Kumasi, 1968.

MIGEOD, F. W. H. *Across Equatorial Africa*. London, 1923.

MINER, HORACE. *The Primitive City of Timbuctoo*. 1953; Garden City, 1965.

OMOKHODION, AKU. "The Beni Culture." M. S. thesis, Kumasi, 1967.

PARK, MUNGO. *Travels and Discoveries in the Interior of Africa*. Vol. 1. London, 1795.

PIGAFETTA, FILIPPO. A *Report of the Kingdom of Congo*. M. Hutchinson, trans. 1591; reprinted New York, 1969.

PINKERTON, JOHN, ed. *Voyages and Travels in All Parts of the World*. Vol. 16. London, 1814.

ROSCOE, JOHN. *The Buganda*. New York, 1911.

ROWE, JOHN ALAN. "Revolution in Buganda." Ph.D. diss., U. of Wisconsin, 1966.

SCHAPERA, I., ed. *Livingstone's Private Journals 1851–1853*. Los Angeles, 1960.

SCHULTZE, A. *The Sultanate of Bornu*. London, 1913.

SELOUS, F. C. *Travel and Adventure in South-East Africa*. London, 1893.

SMITH, WILLIAM. A *New Voyage to Guinea*. 1744; reprinted New York, 1967.

SPEKE, J. H. *Journal of the Discovery of the Nile*. London, 1863.

STANLEY, H. M. *Through the Dark Continent*. Vol. 1. New York, 1879.

———. *In Darkest Africa*. Vol. 1. New York, 1890.

———. *In Darkest Africa*. Vol. 2. London, 1891.

THOMPSON, MATABELE. *An Autobiography*. London, n.d.

THOMSON, JOSEPH. *To the Central African Lakes and Back*. Vol. 2. London, 1881.

TYLER, JOSIAH. *Forty Years among the Zulu*. 1891; reprinted Cape Town, 1971.

WALLIS, J. P. R., ed. *The Matabele Journals of Robert Moffat 1829–1860*. Vol. 1. London, 1965.

WILMOT, A. *Monomotapa*. London, 1896.

WOLF, JAMES B., ed. *Missionary to Tanganyika 1877–1888*. London, 1971.

II. Secondary Sources

ABRAHAMS, R. G. "The Peoples of Greater Nyamwezi, Tanzania," *Ethnographic Survey of Africa*. Vol. 17. London, 1967.

ADAMSON, P. B. "The City Walls of Kano," *Antiquity* 24 (1950).

ADE AJAYI, J. F., and ESPIE, IAN, eds. *A Thousand Years of West African History*. Ibadan, 1965.

ADE AJAYI, J. F., and CROWDER, MICHAEL, eds. *History of West Africa*. Vol. 1. New York, 1972.

———. *History of West Africa*. Vol. 2. New York, 1973.

ADELEYE, R. A. *Power and Diplomacy in Northern Nigeria 1804–1906*. New York, 1971.

AKINOLA, R. A. "Urban Tradition in Yorubaland," *Nigeria Magazine* 95 (December 1967).

ANTUBAM, KOFI. *Ghana's Heritage of Culture*. Leipzig, 1963.

BALANDIER, GEORGES. *Daily Life in the Kingdom of the Kongo*. London, 1968.

BEIER, ULLI. *African Mud Sculpture*. London, 1963.

BELLO, AHMADU. *My Life*. Cambridge, 1962.

BENNETT, N. R., and McCALL, DANIEL, eds. *Aspects of West African Islam*. Vol. 5. Boston, 1971.

BENNETT, NORMAN R. *Mirambo of Tanzania c. 1840–1884*. London, 1971.

BERG, F. J., and WALTER, B. J. "Mosques, Population and Urban Development in Mombasa," *Hadith* 1, (1968).

BERNUS, EDMOND. "Un type d'habitat ancien en Côte d'Ivoire," *Cahiers d'Outre-Mer* 17, no. 65 (1964).

BERRY, L., ed. *Tanzania in Maps*. New York, 1972.

BIOBAKU, S. O., ed. *Sources of Yoruba History*. Oxford, 1973.

BLAKE, J. W., ed. *Europeans in West Africa*. London, 1942.

BOAHEN, ADU. *Topics in West African History*. London, 1966.

———, ed. *Horizon History of Africa*. New York, 1971.

BOHANNAN, LAURA, and BOHANNAN, PAUL. "The Tiv of Central Nigeria," *Ethnographic Survey of Africa*. Vol. 8. London, 1962.

BOVILL, E. W. *The Golden Trade of the Moors*. London, 1958.

BRASSEUR, GÉRARD. *Les établissements humains au Mali*. IFAN, Dakar, 1968.

BUXTON, DAVID. *The Abyssinians*, New York, 1970.

CATON-THOMPSON, G. *Zimbabwe Culture*. London, 1931.

CLARIDGE, W. WALTON. *History of the Gold Coast and Ashanti*. 1915; reprinted New York, 1964.

COLLINS, R. O., ed. *African History: Text and Readings*. New York, 1971.

DAAKU, K. Y. *Trade and Politics on the Gold Coast 1600–1720*. London, 1970.

DANEEL, M. L. *The God of the Matopo Hills*. The Hague, 1970.

DARK, PHILIP J. C. *An Introduction to Benin Art and Technology*. Oxford, 1973.

DAVIDSON, BASIL. *The Lost Cities of Africa*. Boston, 1959.

DAVIDSON, BASIL, ed. *The African Past*. New York, 1967.

DAVIES, OLIVER. *West Africa before the Europeans*. London, 1967.

DIKE, K. O. *Trade and Politics in the Niger Delta, 1830–1885*. Oxford, 1956.

DOUGLAS, MARY, and KABERRY, P. M., eds. *Man in Africa*. London, 1969.

Du BOIS, FELIX. *Timbuctoo the Mysterious*. London, 1896.

Du CHAILLU, P. B. *A Journey to Ashango-Land*. London, 1867.

EKUNDARE, R. O. *An Economic History of Nigeria 1860–1960*. New York 1973.

FAGG, BERNARD *et al. Colloquium on Negro Art, Society of African Culture*. Dakar, 1968.

FORDE, DARYLL., ed. *African Worlds*. London, 1968.

FORDE, DARYLL, and KABERRY, P. M., eds. *West African Kingdoms in the Nineteenth Century*. London, 1967.

FRASER, DOUGLAS. *Village Planning in the Primitive World*. New York, 1968.

FREEMAN-GRENVILLE, G. S. P., ed. and trans. *The East African Coast: Select Documents*. London, 1962.

FROBENIUS, LEO. *The Voice of Africa*. Vol. 1. London, 1913.

FYFE, CHRISTOPHER. *A Short History of Sierra Leone*. London, 1962.

GARLAKE, PETER S. *The Early Islamic Architecture of the East African Coast*. Nairobi, 1966.

———. *Great Zimbabwe*. London, 1973.

GERMOND, R. C., ed. and trans. *Chronicles of Basutoland*. Morija, 1967.

GODDARD, S. "Town-Farm Relationships in Yorubaland," *Africa* 35, no. 1 (1965).

GRAY, J. M. "The Kibuga of Buganda," *Uganda Journal* 25, no. 1 (1961).

GRAY, RICHARD, and BIRMINGHAM, DAVID, eds. *Pre-Colonial African Trade*. New York, 1970.

GREEN, M. M. *Ibo Village Affairs*. 1947; New York, 1964.

GROVE, DAVID. *The Towns of Ghana*. Accra, 1964.

GUTKIND, P. C. W. "Town Life in Buganda," *Uganda Journal* 20, no. 1 (1956).

———. "Notes on the Kibuga of Buganda," *Uganda Journal* 24, no. 1 (1960).

GUTKIND, PETER C. W. *The Royal Capital of Buganda.* The Hague, 1963.

HASELBERGER, HERTA. "Le Tata De Samory en 1886–1887," *Notes Africaines,* 114 (April 1967).

HISKETT, MERVYN. *The Sword of Truth.* London, 1973.

HODGKIN, THOMAS, ed. *Nigerian Perspectives.* London, 1960.

HOGBEN, S. J., and KIRK-GREENE, A. M. *The Emirates of Northern Nigeria.* London, 1966.

HULL, RICHARD W. *Munyakare African Civilization before the Batuuree.* New York, 1972.

JOHNSTON, H. A. S. *The Fulani Empire of Sokoto.* London, 1967.

JOHNSTON, J. P. "Notes on some Stonewall Kraals in South Africa," *Man* 12, no.˙1 (1912).

JONES, EMRYS. *Towns and Cities.* London, 1966.

Journal of the Town Planning Institute 56, no. 5 (1970).

KIRKMAN, JAMES. *Gedi the Palace.* London, 1963.

KRAPF-ASKARI, EVA. *Yoruba Towns and Cities.* Oxford, 1969.

KUPER, ADAM. *Kalahari Village Politics.* London, 1970.

La FONTAINE, J. S. "The Gisu of Uganda," *Ethnographic Survey of Africa.* Vol. 10. London, 1959.

LAST, MURRAY. *The Sokoto Caliphate.* New York, 1967.

LATHAM, A. J. H. *Old Calabar 1600–1891.* Oxford, 1973.

LEVTZION, NEHEMIAH. *Ancient Ghana and Mali.* London, 1973.

LEWIS, I. M., and FORDE, D. eds. *Islam in Tropical Africa.* London, 1966.

LLOYD, P. C., *et al.,* eds. *The City of Ibadan.* Cambridge, 1967.

LOGAN, PHILIP N. "The Walled City of Kano," Journal of British Architects 36, no. 10 (1929).

MABOGUNJE, AKIN L. *Yoruba Towns.* Ibadan, 1962.

———. *Urbanization in Nigeria.* 1968; New York, 1971.

MacDONALD, ALISTER. *Conference on Tropical Architecture.* London, 1953.

MAIR, LUCY. *African Societies.* London, 1974.

MAUNY, RAYMOND. *Tableau géographique de l'ouest africain au Moyen Age.* Dakar, 1961.

———. *Les siècles obscurs de l'Afrique noire.* Paris, 1966.

McHARG, IAN L. *Design with Nature.* Garden City, N.Y., 1971.

MEEK, C. K. *The Northern Tribes of Nigeria.* London, 1925.

MIRACLE, MARVIN. *Agriculture in the Congo Basin.* Madison, Wis., 1967.

MOFFAT, ROBERT. *Matabele Journals,* 2 vols. London, 1945.

MORGAN, W. B., and PUGH, J. C. *West Africa.* London, 1969.

MUMFORD, LEWIS. *The City in History.* New York, 1961.

NADEL, S. F. *A Black Byzantium.* London, 1942.

Nangodi Report No. 2. Faculty of Architecture, Kumasi, 1965.

National Capital Master Plan of Dar es Salaam. Project Planning Associates, Toronto, 1968.

National Research Council. *Housing and Building in Hot Dry Climates.* Washington, D.C., 1953.

NEWMAN, JAMES L. *The Ecological Basis for Subsistence Change among the Sandwe of Tanzania.* Washington, D.C., 1970.

NSIMBI, M. S. "Village Life and Customs in Buganda," *Uganda Journal* 20, no. 1 (1956).

OAKLEY, DAVID. *Tropical Houses.* London, 1961.

OGOT, B. A., and KIERAN, J. A., eds. *Zamani: A Survey of East African History.* New York, 1968.

OJO, G. J. A. *Yoruba Palaces.* London, 1966.

OLIVER, PAUL, ed. *Shelter in Africa.* New York, 1971.

OLIVER, ROLAND. "Ancient Capital Sites of Ankole," *Uganda Journal* 23, no. 1 (1959).

OLIVER, ROLAND, and MATHEW, GERVASE, eds. *History of East Africa.* Vol. 1. Oxford, 1963.

OMER-COOPER, J. D. *The Zulu Aftermath.* Evanston, Ill., 1966.

OTTENBERG, SIMON, ed. *Cultures and Societies of Africa.* New York, 1960.

PADEN, JOHN. "Situational Ethnicity in Urban Africa with Special Reference to the Hausa," unpublished ms., 1972.

POSNANSKY, MERRICK. "The Excavation of an Ankole Capital Site at Bweyorere," *Uganda Journal* 32, no. 2 (1968).

———, ed. *Prelude to East African History.* Nairobi, 1966.

PROTHERO, R. M., and BARBOUR, K. M., eds. *Essays on African Population.* London, 1961.

PROYART, ABBÉ. *History of Loango.* London, 1776.

PRUSSIN, LABELLE. *Architecture in Northern Ghana.* Los Angeles, 1969.

———. "An Introduction to Indigenous African Architecture," *Journal of the Society of Architectural Historians* 33, no. 3 (1974).

RANDLES, W. G. L. *L'ancien royaume du Congo.* Paris, 1968.

RATTRAY, R. S. *Ashanti.* 1923; reprinted New York, 1969.

READE, WINWOOD. *The Story of the Ashantee Campaign.* London, 1874.

RICHARDS, AUDREY I. *The Changing Structure of a Ganda Village.* Nairobi, 1966.

ROBERTS, ANDREW, ed. *Tanzania before 1900.* Nairobi, 1968.

RODNEY, WALTER. "Gold and Slaves on the Gold Coast," *Transactions of the Historical Society of Ghana,* 10 (1969).

ROTH, H. LING. *Great Benin.* 1903; reprinted New York, 1968.

RUDOFSKY, BERNARD. *Architecture without Architects.* Garden City, 1965.

RYDER, ALAN. *Benin and the Europeans 1485–1897.* New York, 1969.

SAUNDERS, CHRISTOPHER, and DERRICOURT, ROBIN, eds. *Beyond the Cape Frontier*. London, 1974.

SHINNIE, MARGARET. *Ancient African Kingdoms*. London, 1965.

SHINNIE, P. L. "Excavations at Bigo," *Uganda Journal* 24, no. 1 (1960).

———. *Meroe*. New York, 1967.

———, ed. *The African Iron Age*. Oxford, 1971.

SIDDLE, D. J. "War-Towns in Sierra Leone," *Africa* 38, no. 1 (1968).

SIMMS, RUTH P. *Urbanization in West Africa*. Evanston, Ill., 1965.

SMITH, ROBERT S. *Kingdoms of the Yoruba*. London, 1969.

STANLEY, RICHARD, and NEAME, ALAN, eds. *The Exploration Diaries of H. M. Stanley*. London, 1961.

STRANDES, JUSTUS. *The Portuguese Period in East Africa*. 1899; Nairobi, reprinted 1961.

SUMMERS, ROGER. *Ancient Ruins and Vanished Civilisations of Southern Africa*. Cape Town, 1971.

SURET-CANALE, J. *Histoire De L'Afrique Occidentale*. Paris, 1965.

Tamale/Kumbungu Survey. Faculty of Architecture, Kumasi, 1970.

THEAL, G. McCALL. *History of South Africa*. Vol. 5. 1908; Cape Town, 1964.

THOMAS, IOAN. "The Flat-Roofed Houses of the Sebei at Benet," *Uganda Journal* 27, no. 1 (1963).

THOMPSON, L., and FERGUSON, J., eds. *Africa in Classical Antiquity*. Ibadan, 1969.

THOMPSON, L. M., ed. *African Societies in Southern Africa*. New York, 1969.

TORDOFF, WILLIAM. *Ashanti under the Prempehs*. London, 1965.

TRIMINGHAM, J. SPENCER. *A History of Islam in West Africa*. 1962; London, 1970.

UCKO, PETER J., *Man, Settlement and Urbanism*. London, 1973.

VANSINA, JAN. *Kingdoms of the Savanna*. Madison, Wis., 1968.

———. *The Tio Kingdom of the Middle Congo 1880–1892*. London, 1973.

WALTON, JAMES. *African Village*. Pretoria, 1956.

WHEATLEY, PAUL. *The Pivot of the Four Corners*. Chicago, 1971.

WILLETT, FRANK. *African Art*. New York, 1971.

———. *Ife in the History of West African Sculpture*. London, 1967.

WILSON, MONICA, and THOMPSON, L. M., eds. *The Oxford History of South Africa*. Vol. 1. Oxford, 1969.

WOLFSON, FREDA, ed. *Pageant of Ghana*. London, 1958.

INDEX